Comprehension and English Language Learners

25 Oral Reading Strategies That Cross Proficiency Levels

Michael F. Opitz
with **Lindsey Moses**

FOREWORD BY David E. Freeman
AND Yvonne S. Freeman

HEINEMANN
Portsmouth, NH

Heinemann
145 Maplewood Ave. Suite 300
Portsmouth, NH 03801
www.heinemann.com

Offices and agents throughout the world

Library of Congress Cataloging-in-Publication Data
Opitz, Michael F.
  Comprehension and English language learners : 25 oral reading strategies that cross proficiency levels / Michael F. Opitz, with Lindsey Moses; foreword by David E. Freeman and Yvonne S. Freeman.
      p. cm.
  Includes bibliographical references.
  ISBN-13: 978-0-325-02678-7
  ISBN-10: 0-325-02678-5
  1. English language—Study and teaching (Elementary)—Foreign speakers. 2. Reading comprehension. I. Moses, Lindsey. II. Title.

PE1128.A2O67 2009
372.47—dc22   2009008394

Editor: Kate Montgomery
Production: Vicki Kasabian
Interior and cover designs: Night & Day Design
Typesetter: Kim Arney
Manufacturing: Steve Bernier

Printed in the United States of America on acid-free paper
5 6 7 8 9   GP   27 26 25 24 23
Digitally Printed GP July 2023
PO 4500876648

To the first Michael Opitz, my grandfather,
an English language learner who
emigrated from Austria to America
through Ellis Island.
—MFO

To my grandmother, Daisy Lazetich,
the first English language
learner I ever loved.
—LM

Contents

Foreword

Comprehension and English Language Learners by Michael Opitz provides teachers with twenty-five oral reading strategies to use with their English language learners (ELLs). Teachers face the daunting task of helping all their students, including their ELLs, develop high levels of literacy. As a result, many teachers have focused much of their instruction on reading and writing. While students need to be able to comprehend grade-level texts and write narratives, reports, and other kinds of academic papers, literacy development also depends crucially on students' development of oral English proficiency. *Comprehension and English Language Learners* gives teachers concrete suggestions for building oral language through meaningful reading activities.

Many teachers are familiar with other books Michael Opitz has written, such as *Rhymes and Reasons, Good-bye Round Robin, Reaching Readers, Do-able Differentiation,* and *Don't Speed. READ!* He has partnered with other literacy leaders in writing several of these books and others. The practical ideas and literature suggestions included in his other books are useful resources for any teachers. However, in *Comprehension and English Language Learners* Opitz, working with Lindsey Moses, has written a book focused squarely on English language learners.

This book comes at a time when the number of ELLs has increased to the point where nearly every teacher needs strategies for working effectively with students who are developing oral and reading skills in English. In the ten years between 1995–96 and 2005–06, the numbers of ELLs in K–12 schools grew over 57 percent to more than five million. This growth compared with only a 3.6 percent growth of the overall school population. And the growth is not only concentrated in a few states. In fact, the largest growth has not been in traditionally high ELL population states such as California, Florida, New York, and Texas, but in states in the southeast like Alabama and Mississippi, and Midwestern states like Nebraska and Colorado. These states all have experienced a 200 percent growth in ELLs (OELA 2007).

It is also important to be aware that not all ELLs are new to this country. While the immigrant population in the U.S. grew by 14 million in the 1990s and is expected to grow another 14 million in the next few years, many ELLs in our schools were born here (Capps, Fix, et al. 2007). Research shows that large numbers, up to 57 percent of the ELLs in secondary schools, are students who were born here and attended school here but still struggle academically. All these demographics highlight why it is important that teachers understand how to help their second language learners develop English from an early age, and Michael Opitz's books are meant to do just that.

English language learners need to develop oral English proficiency as they learn to read and write in English. The National Reading Panel Report (National Institute of Child Health and Human Development 2000), which reviewed literacy research on native English speakers, set the guidelines for much of the instruction children receive in schools. Since that report only looked at native English speakers, a second study was conducted to review the research in literacy for English language learners. This second report, *Developing Literacy in Second-Language Learners* (August and Shanahan 2006), was carried out by the National Literacy Panel.

One of the important findings of the National Literacy Panel report was that the development of oral language is important for growth in reading and writing. As the authors of the report state, "For language-minority learners, oral language proficiency plays an important role in the acquisition of skilled reading" (August and Shanahan 2006, 55). In particular, the oral language development was shown to correlate with reading comprehension. In the chapter of the report on second-language oral proficiency and second-language literacy, the panel notes, "Overall, studies of English-language learners in elementary school have found consistently that oral language proficiency in English and English reading comprehension are positively correlated" (133). These studies all point to the importance of helping ELLs develop oral language skills in English as they learn to read and write in English.

ELLs come to school with differing levels of oral and written English. All ELLs need oral language development, but an oral reading strategy designed to help a newcomer who speaks little or no English would not be appropriate for an ELL who's at a more advanced stage. While teachers can modify good strategies and use them with students at different levels, it is helpful to be provided with strategies geared to the specific proficiency levels. *Comprehension and English Language Learners* is organized in a way that makes it much easier for teachers to find strategies that match with their students' proficiency levels.

TESOL, the professional organization for teachers of English to speakers of other languages, has published the PreK–12 English Language Proficiency Standards (Gottlieb, Carnuccio, et al. 2006). The standards are organized by different levels of English proficiency. TESOL recognizes five levels: starting, emerging, developing, expanding, and bridging.

Different chapters of *Comprehension and English Language Learners* discuss strategies appropriate for a specific level. For example, one strategy for students at the starting level involves using puppets to retell a story that the teacher has read to the class. Another strategy for starting students has them sing together. These strategies allow ELLs to show what they have comprehended from hearing a story read in English. They can do this without speaking or by using only a few words because the strategies provide the students with props and other ways of responding. In contrast, later chapters present strategies during which ELLs use their greater language proficiency and build their oral language as they engage in various activities. Students at the emerging stage, for instance, may be asked to describe to a partner the mental images they formed as they listened to a passage with vivid descriptive writing.

Opitz explains five strategies for each of the five proficiency levels. The chapters follow the same format. Each chapter starts with a scenario that describes one or more students at a particular level. Then comes a chart that cross-references these five strategies presented with specific reading skills the strategies help students develop. The strategy is first briefly described. The description is followed by a step-by-step list of teaching suggestions. These suggestions clearly outline how to implement the strategy. The strategy is then contextualized in a section called Classroom Conversations. In this section Opitz describes how a teacher uses the strategy with his or her class. For each strategy, Opitz also lists several books appropriate to use with the strategy, related websites, and a short section called Handy Hints. Having this consistent format for each chapter makes the book easy to follow. Teachers can easily find ideas for students at different levels.

English language learners need to develop oral English proficiency as well as the ability to read and write English at the same level as native English speakers. This process takes time. However, teachers can scaffold instruction for their ELLs by engaging them in meaningful literacy activities that involve reading, writing, speaking, and listening. *Comprehension and English Language Learners* gives teachers useful oral reading strategies aligned with the different proficiency levels ELLs move through. Although there are a number of books available for helping ELLs develop their English reading and writing skills, this book is one of the few that focuses on oral language development, a crucial but often overlooked component of academic development for ELLs. As such, it helps fill a gap in the professional resources teachers need to help their English language learners reach high levels of oral and written English proficiency.

—David and Yvonne Freeman

References

August, D., and T. Shanahan, eds. 2006. *Developing Literacy in Second-Language Learners: Report of the National Literacy Panel on Language Minority Children and Youth.* Mahwah, NJ: Lawrence Erlbaum Associates.

Capps, R., M. Fix, et al. 2007. "Immigrant Children, Urban Schools, and the No Child Left Behind Act." www.migrationalinformation .org/feature/display.cfm?ID=347.

Gottleib, M., L. M. Carnuccio, et al. 2006. *PreK–12 English Lanuage Proficiency Standards.* Alexandria, VA: Teachers of English to Speakers of Other Languages.

Krashen, S., and T. Terrell. 1983. *The Natural Approach: Language Acquisition in the Classroom.* Hayward, CA: Alemany Press.

National Institute of Child Health and Human Development. 2000. *Report of the National Reading Panel. Teaching Children to Read: An Evidence-Based Assessment of the Scientific Research Literature on Reading and Its Implications for Instruction.* Washington, D.C.: U.S. Government Printing Office.

Office of English Language Acquisition (OELA). 2007. *The Growing Number of Limited English Proficient Students 1995–96–2005–06.* Washington, D.C.: Office of English Language Acquisition.

Acknowledgments

Many individuals helped me bring this book to fruition. I thank my colleagues at the University of Northern Colorado: Lindsey Moses for her numerous contributions to this text, and Dr. James A. Erekson for coauthoring Chapter 2. My thanks extend to all those extraordinary individuals at Heinemann: Maura Sullivan and Kate Montgomery, who perceived a need for this book and encouraged me to write it; Dr. Yvonne Freeman and Dr. David Freeman, for offering their keen insights and editorial assistance; Berna Faye Bowhan, for brainstorming; Vicki Kasabian, the jovial, meticulous production editor, for making the manuscript look so grand; Eric Chalek for his lucid prose that appears on the back cover of this book; Denise Botelho for copyediting that brought greater clarity to this text; Cindy Black for her eagle-eyed proofreading; and to Night & Day Design for the marvelous cover and interior designs that grace the book you hold in your hands. Finally, I thank Sheryl, my first lady, for her support, patience, and understanding. To all, my heartfelt thanks.

—Michael F. Opitz

I thank Michael Opitz for inviting me to be a part of this project and for his encouragement and support. I would also like to thank my husband, Stephen Guccione, for "coaching me up" with his positive and motivating words. Finally, I thank my parents, Mike and Karen Moses, for being my first teachers and biggest supporters.

—Lindsey Moses

Introduction

*"Okay, Natasha, time for you to go to the fourth grade for reading,"
third-grade teacher Brad reminds. Hearing his reminder, Natasha,
an English language learner (ELL) who reads well above grade
level, gathers the necessary materials and exits with a Tigger-like
gait. As a result of being provided some excellent instruction,
Natasha's first language skills transferred to learning English
with relative ease. And at her current school, where students are
grouped across grades for reading instruction, Natasha reads with
the fourth graders.*

*One hour later, Natasha returns, her Tigger-like manner
replaced with an Eyeore demeanor. Without prompting, she shares,
"Fourth grade reading is s-o-o-o boring!"*

Surprised and curious, Brad asks, "What's so boring about it?"

Hands on hips, Natasha launches into her explanation:
*"Well, all you do is sit in a circle and take turns reading a story you
have never read. One person reads out loud while the rest are supposed to follow along. When that person is finished reading a page,
the next person starts reading. Then after everyone has read one
page, you have to go around the circle again until the story is finished! Then the time is over. You don't even get to talk about the
story or ask others about their ideas. See what I mean? It's s-o-o-o
boring!"*

I do see what Natasha means. What she describes is *round robin reading,* "the outmoded practice of calling on students to read orally one
after the other" (Harris and Hodges 1995, 222).

And I also see that Natasha is an astute learner who knows that
discussing a story is one way to further and deepen one's understanding of it. Finally, Natasha provides evidence that she is able to comprehend and use both conversational and academic English with ease.
Although she is a mere eight years old, she is nevertheless functioning
at the last and most advanced English proficiency level, *bridging.*

Students like Natasha helped me see the need for this book, for while using oral reading teaching strategies to help children advance as readers certainly has its place in the reading curriculum, *round robin reading* does not. How, then, can well-meaning teachers best use oral reading teaching strategies as literacy scaffolds to help all ELLs at all English language proficiency levels advance as readers?

The answer to this question is the aim of this book. I begin by presenting my definition of reading and ten reasons for using oral reading. True, silent reading is used most often both in and out of school thus it needs to remain the primary mode of reading. Still, oral reading has a place in helping children to acquire a greater understanding of how to best comprehend when reading silently and how to communicate this understanding with others. Consider the times when you want to share information you have first read silently with another, such as a saying you have come across, a poem, or a funny anecdote. You will use oral reading to share (e.g., "Hey! You have to listen to this!"). To be sure, all children, ELLs included, need to use both silent and oral reading in order to become proficient readers as I define them in Chapter 1.

Given that ELLs are front and center in this book, I also provide a definition of ELLs, describe the English language proficiency levels through which they advance, and present an overview of the oral reading teaching strategies that are most appropriate for each level. As the chart on pp. 10–11 shows, each strategy is intended to enhance ELLs' comprehension strategies (i.e., listening and reading) and vocabulary (i.e., conversational and academic).

A word of caution is in order here. The whole purpose of identifying levels of language proficiency is to help understand where children are and where they need to be. Helping them advance through the levels effectively and efficiently is the primary mission. The goal is to help them become proficient in both conversational and academic English. Likewise, the descriptions are designed to show general trends rather than discrete attributes that must be mastered before children can be seen as having advanced to the next proficiency level. As Baynham (1993) reminds, language learning is anything but linear. Instead, it fluctuates depending on the task and context at hand. Clearly, what is most important is being able to use language for a variety of purposes, both conversational and academic, rather than taking on a label.

But how will you know if children are becoming proficient? In Chapter 2, Effective Oral Reading Assessment Strategies for English Language Learners, colleague James Erekson and I provide some answers to this most important question. As you will discover, in order to best assess children, we need to ask and answer three questions: *What do I want to know? Why do I want to know it? How can I best discover this information?* Questions asked and answered leads to selecting and using specific assessment techniques that will help you to tease out what children know and need to know in order to continue their growth as ELLs. An interpretation of students' performance on the different assessments then guides selecting the most appropriate oral reading strategy and using it in the ensuing instruction.

Fortunately, there are several effective ways of using oral reading with ELLs who appear to be functioning at various levels of English language proficiency. They form the content of Chapters 3 through 7. In each chapter, I showcase five specific oral reading teaching strategies that elicit and enable specific language competencies. Each chapter follows a similar format. I begin with a brief description of the English language proficiency level the given chapter showcases. I then provide five teaching strategies best suited to that stage. Each teaching strategy includes a description, teaching suggestions, sample appropriate children's literature titles, teacher and children's voices to show how teachers use the strategy and how children respond to it, related websites, and some additional ways that the strategy can be used and modified.

Although Chapters 3 through 7 are written as stand-alone chapters, keep in mind that many of the strategies cut across the various stages. *Teacher Read-Aloud*, for example, is showcased in Chapter 3 as a way to help children in the *starting* level. Nevertheless, it can be used at other levels, too. In other words, the strategies are presented as they are to help busy teachers access those that are *best* suited to a given proficiency level; there is nonetheless some overlap.

As a result of reading and using the suggestions herein, I am confident that you will see for yourself that there are many advantages to using these oral reading teaching strategies as scaffolds to help ELLs become increasingly better readers of English. You'll agree that reading in general, and oral reading in particular, doesn't have to be, in Natasha's words, "s-o-o-o boring!" See what I mean?

Understanding Reading and English Language Learners

Walk into any bookstore and you are sure to see people of all ages reading a variety of texts. Most will be reading to themselves and, on occasion, will share what they consider to be an interesting part with others who are in their company. Having used silent reading to comprehend the material, the readers use oral reading to communicate their understanding. So while both silent and oral reading have their place, if you watch long enough, you'll see that silent reading takes precedence over oral reading. And this is as it should be for the majority of reading in everyday life is done silently.

Given that silent reading reigns supreme in everyday reading outside of school, and given that, like you, I want to help children understand what and how readers truly interact with text, why offer you a text that emphasizes oral reading in school? And why do I steer you clear of *round robin reading* for all children, ELLs in particular? Answers to these questions form the foundation and structure of this chapter. Explaining my definition of reading seems a good place to begin as it provides necessary grounding for the remaining questions in this chapter and for the remainder of this text.

What Is Reading?

Ask different reading researchers this question, and you are sure to get a variety of answers. In fact, Harris and Hodges (1995) and Tracy and Morrow (2006) offer several definitions of reading each reflecting different models created by theorists to explain the reading process. My definition draws on the research of several individuals and, as Figure 1–1 shows, is multifaceted. It includes five distinct but related components that proficient readers use when reading (Kucer 2005). Proficient readers:

1. *Read with comprehension.* Comprehension is the essence of reading and readers are both active and purposeful in their quest to construct meaning. In fact, they do a lot more. They look over a text before they read making some predictions about the text and determine their purpose for reading it. They then read selectively, decid-

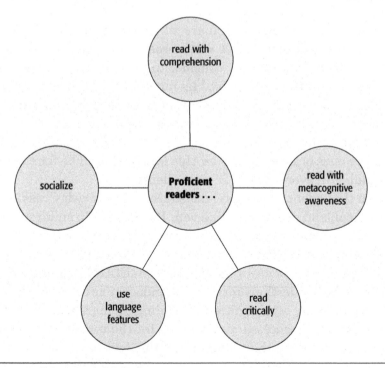

Figure 1–1. Proficient Reader Behaviors

ing which parts need to be read more slowly or more quickly depending on their background knowledge of the text and their purpose for reading it. They summarize as they read making sure that they are able to remember specific information or make an accurate interpretation of the author's intended meaning. In other words, they are thoughtful, strategic readers (Duke and Pearson 2002).

2. *Read with metacognitive awareness.* Comprehension sometimes breaks down. Proficient readers recognize when this happens. Rather than give up on the text, they determine where the breakdown occurred and what they might do to get back on track. If the problem is not knowing the meaning of a word, for example, these readers may decide to continue reading to see if the coming text will clarify the meaning. They might also choose to reread the text with the unknown word to determine if the context of the sentence lends understanding.

3. *Read critically.* Critical reading is "reading in which a questioning attitude, logical analysis, and inference are used to judge the worth of text according to an established standard" (Harris and Hodges 1995, 47). As the definition suggests, readers' judgments are anything but mere opinion. Instead, readers have some external or internal standards that form their judgments. For instance, they might have additional information about the topic at hand that they use to evaluate the current text. Critical reading calls on readers to suspend their judgments while they consider several viewpoints. Readers must go beyond any one text to judge what they have read. Verifying factual statements, distinguishing between facts and opinions, judging sources of information, and identifying propaganda techniques are but four critical reading skills.

4. *Socialize.* A big part of reading is talking with the author when reading. Evidence of this "talking" can be found in the notes that readers make to themselves either in the margins of the text or on another piece of paper when reading. But readers also talk with others at different phases of reading to develop a fuller understanding of a text and to gain different perspectives. *Before reading*, readers might discuss what they know about the material, making a list of their collective thoughts. *During reading*, readers might stop and ask another reader what they think is going on in the text and what they think the author seeks to convey. *After reading*, readers often discuss what they took away from the text. Discussions such as these often lead readers to see different perspectives and different interpretations of the text because more often than not, different readers see different ideas based on their prior experiences.

5. *Use language features.* Readers are constantly asking themselves three questions as they read: "Does this make sense?" "Does this sound right?" "Does this look right?" These three questions are an indication that readers are intuitively using three linguistic cueing systems as they read: semantic, syntactic, and graphophonic. They derive semantic cues from the text's meaning, syntactic cues from the text's grammatical structure, and graphophonic from sound/symbol relationships and patterns. All of these work together to help readers construct meaning.

Finally, readers use *pragmatics* (i.e., the context in which they are reading) and the type of reading material to guide what and how they read. They might choose to read one type of text when at home and another when they are with friends. Likewise, they read the text in different ways depending on their purpose for reading. If they are trying to ascertain important details from the text, for example, they might read in a more study-like fashion, underlining important points. On the other hand, if they are reading to share some of the content with friends, they might skim the text for highlights.

Who Are English Language Learners?

English language learners (ELLs) are those who are fortunate to know a language other than English. In fact, sometimes these learners may know more than one language. Regardless, the language they seek to acquire is English, hence the label *English language learner*. ELLs are constantly showing what they know and what they need to learn. As such, there is much variability among them, not to be confused with disability (Roller 1996).

Researchers have identified different levels of language proficiency through which language learners progress (Krashen and Terrell 1983).

Figure 1–2 draws on these initial delineations of levels as well as others' adaptations of them (e.g., Freeman and Freeman 2000; Kendal and Khuon 2005). These levels, as delineated in the TESOL standards (2006), are described briefly and include some implications for how oral reading can best be used to help learners in the specific stage. But be forewarned! When learning a new language, any individual, regardless of age, progresses through these levels. To assume that the levels coincide with a specific grade level is problematic.

Levels of Language Proficiency	Description	Implications for Using Oral Reading
Level 1: Starting	Students have a limited understanding of English. They may respond using nonverbal cues in an attempt to communicate basic needs. They begin to imitate others and use some single words or simple phrases.	The teacher and other more advanced students should model oral reading. Students in the starting level should not be forced to speak, but should be given the opportunity to participate in a group activity where they won't be singled out.
Level 2: Emerging	Students are beginning to understand some phrases and simple sentences. They respond using memorized words and phrases.	Teacher and students should continue tinue to model oral reading. Students should be encouraged to begin taking taking risks with simple, rehearsed oral reading in nonthreatening situations.
Level 3: Developing	Students' listening comprehension improves, and they can understand written English. Students are fairly comfortable engaging in social conversations using simple sentences, but they are just beginning to develop their academic language proficiency.	Students continue to learn through modeling. Students should be participating in whole-class, small-group, partner, and rehearsed oral reading activities. They will need support and opportunities to practice with feedback before doing independent or paired oral reading for an audience.

continues

Figure 1–2. Levels of Language Proficiency, Descriptions, and Implications

Levels of Language Proficiency	Description	Implications for Using Oral Reading
Level 4: Expanding	Students understand and frequently use conversational English with relatively high accuracy. They are able to communicate their ideas in both oral and written contexts. They are also showing the ability to use academic vocabulary.	With scaffolding, students can sucessfully participate in most oral reading activities that native speakers are expected to complete. Using open-ended questions allows students to demonstrate comprehension and academic language development.
Level 5: Bridging	Students comprehend and engage in conversational and academic English with proficiency. They perform at or near grade level in reading, writing, and other content areas.	Students should be encouraged to use higher-level thinking skills during their oral reading. They are near nativelike proficiency in oral reading, but may still need support with analyzing, inferring, evaluating, and reading critically.

Figure 1–2. *Continued*

Also problematic is seeing language learning as a linear process. As Freeman and Freeman (2007) make clear, it is anything but linear. When using language in less formal settings, such as when having conversations with friends, ELLs may demonstrate that they have acquired *Basic Interpersonal Communicative Skills* (BICS) and, as such, be functioning at level 5 (*bridging*), the most advanced level of language acquisition. However, these same learners can and do have difficulty using language in more formal settings such as school. They may demonstrate that they are functioning at level 3 (*developing*), the third level of language proficiency. They need assistance in acquiring academic language. In other words, these ELLs need help in acquiring *Cognitive Academic Language Proficiency* (CALP). Without a doubt, then, the same children who appear to be functioning at a given level are instead functioning at different levels depending on how they are called on to use language.

Why Use Oral Reading with English Language Learners?

Trying to communicate with Russian educators who were visiting my campus helped me to better understand the four factors that McCauley and McCauley (1992) cite as necessary for acquiring a second language: a low-anxiety environment, repeated practice, comprehensible input, and drama. A variety of activities ensued to help all, American and Russian alike, better understand one another. Through the many scheduled activities, which included tours, dinners, presentations, language games, singing, and dancing, one overarching theme cut across them making for a low-anxiety environment: acceptance. And through these varied activities, I was provided with repeated practice, which helped me to acquire some Russian words. Finally, the activities served as different scaffolds that provided comprehensible input, enabling me to comprehend.

Make no mistake! I make no claim to be an expert at speaking and listening, let alone reading and writing, Russian. But what I do claim is that the experience brought to life just how important it is to structure learning so that learners can succeed. Like others (Bruner 1978; Vygotsky 1978), I think of this type of support structure as a *scaffold*. Most often associated with construction workers, scaffolds are temporary platforms builders use when working on buildings that are too tall to reach from the ground. At other times, the scaffolds enable workers to work more efficiently. Rather than climbing up and down a ladder and having to move a ladder when applying stucco, for example, workers can load all necessary materials on the scaffold and stand in place. The scaffolds make the work less strenuous. Once completed, the scaffold is removed.

The same can be said for acquiring a new language, in this case, English. Years ago, Boyle and Peregoy (1990, 152) went so far as to define criteria of literacy scaffolds. Their five criteria still hold true.

Literacy scaffolds

1. Are applied to reading and writing activities aimed at functional, meaningful communication found in whole texts, such as stories, poems, reports, and recipes.

2. Make use of language and discourse patterns that repeat themselves and are, therefore, predictable.

3. Provide a model, offered by the teacher or by peers, for comprehending and producing particular written language patterns.

4. Support students in comprehending and providing written language at a level slightly beyond their competence in the absence of the scaffold.

5. Are temporary and may be dispensed with when the student is ready to work without them.

Oral reading, then, is one such scaffold and the twenty-five different teaching strategies within this book are variations of it. In other words, while oral reading is used in all of the teaching strategies, the way it plays out and the level of support it provides varies. When using *Say It with the Puppet* (p. 46), for instance, teachers enable learners to use conversational language to convey ideas. When using *Find the Signs* (p. 96), teachers provide comprehensible input by showing students how punctuation and other typographical cues signal the author's intended meaning. In both cases, once students show that they can work without the scaffolds, they are removed. Oral reading is not the end. It is the means to the end, which is being able to read independently with understanding.

Beyond this more general reason for using oral reading, though, are ten more specific reasons.

1. *To whet ELLs' appetites for reading.* I can think of few ways to excite ELLs about reading than by reading to them. In addition to helping them develop an ear for another language, I can show them that different authors use different words and texts to covey their ideas. I can also show them that reading is an enjoyable experience. Through this reading, I can invite them to join the literacy club (Smith 1986).

2. *To help ELLs acquire language proficiencies in authentic contexts.* In order to acquire a language, learners need to use it. They need to be actively engaged so that they can make the meaningful connections that are necessary for learning. When using *How Do I Feel?* (p. 101), for example, teachers provide students with an opportunity to experience how authors use words to show how characters feel. Inviting students to talk about feelings that they may have in common with the character(s) provides a vehicle for students to use conversational English, thereby gaining greater language facility (i.e., BICS). Likewise, because learners are sure to be at different levels of growth, a discussion such as this enables students to grow by hearing others talk.

3. *To help ELLs better understand how speaking is related to the other language arts.* So often, it seems as though children acquiring English have little or no understanding of how the different components of language are related. One of the best ways to help them see the connections is to use specific oral reading teaching strategies. *Draw, Tell, and Listen* (p. 80), for example, calls on students to listen to a given section of a story, then draw something that relates to that section. Once completed, students share their drawings and listen to others share theirs. In this one activity, students use all of the language arts for the purpose of communicating with an interested other. As a result of participating in it, they are more likely to see how all components of language are used to communicate with others.

4. *To help ELLs develop social and academic vocabularies.* Several researchers have called attention to the importance of helping ELLs develop both social (i.e., conversational) and academic vocabulary (e.g., Cummins 1979). Halliday's (1975) delineation of the seven ways that children use language illustrates how children use conversational language. Freeman and Freeman (2007) provide greater understanding of academic vocabulary, noting that there are three types: general (those that cut across all content areas), content-specific (those that relate to a specific content area), and signal words (those that show relationships among ideas within a text). Collectively, these researchers emphasize that children need to become flexible language users, those who know how to use language for a variety of purposes and those who feel comfortable enough with the different language forms to do just that. As Figure 1–3 shows, the different

Comprehension and English Language Learners

Reading Skills	Level 1: Starting					Level 2: Emerging				
	Say It with the Puppet	Sing a Song	Read the Pictures	Teacher Read-Aloud	Read Your World	Shared Reading	Fill the Gaps	Draw, Tell, and Listen	Think-Aloud, Think Along, Think Alone	Chime Right In
Positive Attitudes/Interest in Reading	•	•	•	•	•	•	•	•	•	•
Reading Comprehension			•		•	•	•		•	•
Listening Comprehension	•	•		•				•	•	
Social Vocabulary	•	•	•		•			•	•	
Academic Vocabulary		•	•	•	•	•	•		•	•
Use of Language Cues			•		•	•	•		•	
Predicting			•	•			•		•	
Forming Images	•	•	•	•				•		
Using Prior Knowledge			•	•	•		•	•	•	
Monitoring			•			•	•		•	
Inferring	•		•	•			•		•	
Fluency (R = rate, A = accuracy, P = prosody)	P	P		R A P	A	R A P	A			P
Skimming										

Figure 1–3. 25 Effective Oral Reading Strategies and Skills for ELLs

Level 3: Developing					Level 4: Expanding					Level 5: Bridging				
Find the Signs	How Do I Feel?	Read with Me	What's the Word?	Listen to Me	Get the Picture	Readers Theatre	Directed Listening Thinking Activity (DLTA)	Find the Facts	What Does It Mean?	Directed Reading Thinking Activity (DRTA)	Response Quad	Follow the Guide	Poetry Circle	Let's Get Critical
•	•	•	•	•	•	•	•	•	•	•	•	•	•	•
•	•	•			•	•		•	•	•	•	•	•	•
		•	•			•	•				•		•	•
	•	•	•	•	•	•					•		•	•
		•	•	•	•	•	•	•	•	•	•	•		•
•	•	•	•	•	•	•					•	•	•	
			•			•	•		•	•		•		•
					•	•	•						•	
	•		•		•	•		•		•				•
		•		•		•		•		•	•	•		
•	•	•				•		•		•		•		•
P	P	R A P		R A P		R A P					R A P		R A P	
							•					•		

oral reading strategies I include in this book go a long way in helping teachers to attain this goal.

5. *To develop listening comprehension.* In *Listen Hear!* (Opitz and Zbaracki 2004), I devote considerable attention to the value of listening comprehension. As it relates to the discussion here, two points are germane. First, listening comprehension appears to be important for reading comprehension. Learners who are able to listen with comprehension appear to be able to do the same with reading comprehension. Second, if children are to listen better, they need to be taught how. Using oral reading is one of the best and most natural ways to accomplish this teaching. When using a *DLTA* (p. 130), students are given specific information to listen for and also encouraged to make some predictions based on what they have heard and comprehended.

6. *To develop ELLs' reading comprehension.* Perhaps one of the greatest understandings that all learners, ELLs included, need to understand is that authors use a variety of markings to cue readers into the meaning of the text. Beyond specific words, authors use boldface, different punctuation marks, italic print, different print sizes, all to convey an intended meaning. More often than not, children need some explicit instruction that calls attention to these features. Oral reading is a means for doing so. When using *Find the Signs* (p. 96), for instance, teachers can choose a specific text feature and use the text to teach students about it. Students can then be led to identifying and using the given features when reading their independently selected texts.

7. *To assist ELLs in developing positive attitudes and interest in reading.* Perhaps one of the best ways to engender positive attitudes and an interest in reading is to show students as much as tell them. Teachers can show by their expressions and comments that they enjoy reading and that they have specific reading interests. Oral reading provides an excellent way to do just that. Teachers can share with students a book they are currently reading for pleasure, perhaps reading a bit of it to students and commenting on why that passage was selected for reading aloud. On other occasions, teachers can share their favorite stories or poems and let students know why they are favorites. After this modeling, teachers might select *Read with Me* (p. 105) to show students how they can locate and share a favorite with an interested audience.

8. *To determine the strategies ELLs use when reading.* Oral reading provides a window into what the reader is doing when reading silently. True, reading researchers have yet to make a final determination if there is direct transfer to silent reading but for now, it is the assumption most use when using oral reading to assess readers (Allington 1984). As a result of listening in on children's reading, teachers can determine the language cues children use when reading (see Chapter 2) and those who might need further explicit attention. Depending on the focus for the assessment, teachers can use oral reading to determine the fix-up strategies children use when they come to unknown words. But children, too, can assess their own reading. After reading, for example, children can be invited to listen to a self-recording and to do a self-rating. In Chapter 2, I provide specific suggestions for how to use oral reading as an assessment tool.

9. *To provide ELLs with additional reading time necessary for ongoing reading growth.* There is ample evidence to support what seems like common sense: students who read more are better readers (Krashen 2004; Allington 2006). Many of the oral reading teaching strategies enable this meaningful reading time. Consider *Poetry Circle* (p. 162), for example. In an effort to find that perfect poem to share with others in the group, think of the many poems that children need to read! Once selected, children read and reread the poem so that they can share it with others via oral reading with ease and meaning. You get the idea. Much time is spent reading to prepare for the poetry circle.

10. *To address the TESOL Goals and Standards.* TESOL goals and standards call attention to the development of both social communication and academic achievement. They also emphasize the importance of using English in socially and culturally appropriate ways. The oral reading strategies in this book enable ELLs to achieve these goals. When using *How Do I Feel?* (p. 101), for example, ELLs must examine how authors use words to convey ideas about story characters and share their thoughts with classmates. When using *Find the Facts* teachers enhance students' academic achievement (i.e., *CALP*) by expecting them to read and understand content-area material.

Why Not Use Round Robin Reading (aka Popcorn Reading)?

When I think of answering this question, I am reminded of Natasha's emphatic response, "It's s–o-o-o boring!" because it certainly is for more students than not. But beyond this initial response, there are other good reasons for ridding ourselves of this outmoded practice, sometimes disguised as "popcorn reading," which calls on students to pop up and read a nonrehearsed passage when signaled to do so. Did you know, for example, that round robin reading has no research base? Did you also know that no one is certain where round robin reading originated? A graduate student of mine discovered the following quotation from Quintilian's "Institutes of Oratory" (A.D. 95), from which hints at a possible starting point:

> For to me it seems easier, as well as far more advantageous, that the master, after calling for silence, should appoint some one pupil to read, (and it will be best that this duty should be imposed on them by turns,) that they may thus accustom themselves to clear pronunciation. (Bizzell and Herzberg 2001, 374)

With the current emphasis on research and the necessity of using evidence-based best practices to educate children, then, another reason for moving away from round robin reading is that it has no credibility.

But there are still other reasons for moving away from round robin reading. Here are five.

1. *It provides ELLs with an inaccurate view of reading English.* From the onset of instruction, perhaps the greatest learning that teachers need to help ELLs understand is that comprehension, rather than word calling, is what drives reading. Using purposeful oral reading strategies can help lead students to this important understanding whereas round robin reading leads them away from it. As the bookstore scenario that opens this chapter illustrates, readers most often use silent reading in everyday reading. They only use oral reading to accomplish a specific purpose such as when they want to share information or perform. At other times, readers rely on oral reading as a coping strategy. In other words, they may recognize that comprehension has broken down and may decide to read aloud to themselves with the hope that doing so will bring about some understanding. In all of these situations, oral reading is used in an authentic way to accomplish a specific purpose. In contrast, when using round robin reading, students experience oral reading in an artificial way. That is, rarely, if ever, are readers called upon to read an unrehearsed passage in turn while others follow along. And rarely do others correct readers when a stated word does not match the text. Emphasizing unrehearsed reading and correcting misspelled words, which most often occurs when using round robin reading, risks leaving students with an understanding that reading is more about accurate word calling than it is about comprehension, a serious misconception of what constitutes effective reading of English.

2. *It can potentially cause faulty reading habits instead of effective reading strategies.* Readers tend to read at different rates and this variation is natural (Flurkey 2006). Expecting students to follow along while another reads an unrehearsed passage inevitably slows those readers who read at faster rates than the person who is reading aloud. On other occasions, the oral reader reads too quickly leaving students, many ELLs in particular, little or no time to decipher the meaning of unknown words. Instead, they are forced to forge ahead rather than stop and think. In both cases, readers are disenfranchised because they are unable to process information in a manner best suited to them. *All* students need to learn that self-monitoring is important when reading as is paying attention to meaning, recognizing when it breaks down, and what to do about it. The ability to do so is one hallmark of proficient readers as I define them.

3. *It can cause inattentive behaviors, leading to discipline problems.* Those of you who are familiar with round robin reading know the drill. While one student is reading aloud, the others in the group are supposed to follow along—but they rarely do. Instead, they are reading ahead, either because they are interested and want to keep reading, bored and therefore try to do something to alleviate their feelings of boredom, or, as in the case of many ELLs, they are self-conscious of their accent and decide to give themselves some practice time so that when called on they will sound more acceptable to others. Reasons for reading ahead dismissed, what often happens is that students are reprimanded for not following along as told, leaving them with a less-than-favorable view of what it means to come together to share a text. Aside from making students appear unruly, the main problem is that little attention is given to discussing the text at hand. Between the time it takes to read aloud and to reprimand, there is none left for discussing, an important part of the reading experience that enables all to thrive.

4. *It can be a source of anxiety and embarrassment for all students, ELLs in particular.* I have worked with countless teachers who seek to understand best ways to use oral reading that will help students advance as readers. As a part of this work, I more often than not have them experience *round robin reading* firsthand. These teachers admit that they were not following along as told but rather were trying to figure out my pattern of calling on people so that they could figure out what to practice ahead of time to sound good when called on. All comments focus on saving face, not embarrassing themselves. After going through the experience, they better understand how students must feel when called on and what they do to save face when reading in front of others. And this is the major point of the exercise: to show more than tell them how *round robin reading* causes anxiety and embarrassment to appear and that when using it, comprehension is virtually nonexistent.

5. *It consumes valuable classroom time that could be spent on other meaningful activities.* With *round robin reading*, much time is spent trying to keep all students on track and on reading with accuracy. Little if any time is devoted to comprehension. Yet there are many ways to use oral reading in purposeful and meaningful ways such as those shown in this book. Regardless, comprehension is always the goal. Oral reading is merely used as a vehicle to facilitate this comprehension. The objective, then, is not to rid us of oral reading but instead to use it to students' best advantage.

What Are Some Effective Oral Reading Strategies to Use with English Language Learners?

Figure 1–3 shows oral reading teaching strategies designed to help ELLs attain specific skills in authentic contexts. Use it as it was intended: to select and use purposeful and meaningful oral reading teaching strategies as scaffolds to help ELLs become the best possible silent readers of English.

As you read Chapters 3 through 7, please keep these two additional points in mind:

1. Proficiency levels know no grade-level boundaries. Therefore, there are no grade-level distinctions for the various oral reading strategies. Modify them as you see fit to adjust to the unique needs of your students.

2. Picture books, books in which the "illustrations are as important as the text" (Harris and Hodges 1995, 188), reign supreme throughout this book for four reasons. First, many are culturally relevant enabling students to see themselves in texts. Second, the pictures help students to understand the narrative, especially when background for the text is limited. Third, authors use pertinent words to explain ideas. Consequently, students are able to acquire new vocabulary in authentic, meaningful contexts. Fourth, the information appears less daunting than other types of texts (e.g., textbooks), leaving students with feelings of success and a positive association with reading.

Effective Oral Reading Assessment Strategies for English Language Learners

As March settles in, Sharon falls into her observation routine during the daily scheduled independent reading. Her fourth graders have come to expect that Sharon will be watching and conferring with them. Today she observes Nidia and Seth while they read independently. In particular, Sharon is focusing on self-monitoring, letting it guide her observations. What she sees is gratifying. Nidia, who in October was responding to literature with head nods and finger pointing, is monitoring her reading and is now responding with meaningful two- and three-word phrases. And then there's Seth, the boy who in January was saying "so many stuffs" and "so much things," who is now saying "so much stuff" and "so many things." He, too, is showing signs of self-monitoring as Sharon listens in on his reading and hears him make some self-corrections. Sharon makes notes to herself on the observation guide as a way of remembering what she observes.

❖ I thank Dr. James Erekson for his work on this chapter.

Experienced teachers like Sharon understand that observation is one way to detect what students do when they read in authentic contexts. They also know that there are several other appropriate instruments for assessing ELLs' reading and that they are not so different from those they use with the rest of their students. With ELLs, for instance, miscue analyses, student self-assessments, and observational instruments are effective tools. How teachers think about these assessments and even how they administer them often changes, depending on the student's English proficiency level. Despite these differences, one constant holds true: assessment informs and guides instructional decision making. The purpose of this chapter is to highlight some of these informal assessment strategies and call attention to how they can best be used with ELLs. In Figure 2–1, I use three questions to frame the assessment strategies I showcase in this chapter: *What Do I Want to Know? Why Do I Want to Know It? How Can I Best Discover It?*

In addition to these strategies, each of the twenty-five oral reading strategies in Chapter 3 through 7 incorporate some form of informal assessment in that each requires students to generate some kind of performance or artifact. Regardless of the informal assessment strategy, the following three principles hold true.

Principle 1: Take the ELL's Perspective

Learning to see the difference between everyday social language (BICS) and academic language (CALP) is one key way to take the ELL's perspective. The language ELLs encounter in text and in the classroom is not the same language they learn with friends and family. When children see a word such as *difficult* in a text, for example, they may not have had much experience with the academic version of the everyday word *hard*.

Using a simple chart for categorizing words and phrases based on when and how language learners use them is one way to monitor BICS and CALP distinctions (see Figures 2–2 and 2–3). Directions for completing the chart are at the bottom of Figure 2–3.

Having completed the activity, you most likely discovered for yourself that these sets of words demonstrate not only synonyms but also words with different connotations. The difference between how the

What Do I Want to Know?	Why Do I Want to Know It?	How Can I Best Discover It?
Do the students understand when I read aloud to the class?	Comprehension is the goal of reading activities. If my read-alouds are not comprehensible to ELLs, I want to know how to make them more understandable.	Total physical response (TPR), pp. 27–28 Questioning (verbal response), pp. 28–29 Response to literature with drawing, p. 30
Does the student have authentic purposes for reading?	Since skills are most likely taught explicitly in early grades, I want to know whether the ELL is also developing real-life reasons to read (pleasure, information).	Observational checklists, p. 25 Anecdotal records during free reading times, p. 26
Why does the student miscue on particular sounds, even after phonics instruction?	I want to know whether the student has a problem with phonics, or whether it is simple influence from home language.	Contrastive analysis between first language and English, pp. 31–33
Do students who read words well also understand what they read?	Because some ELLs learn the phonics system before they gain vocabulary, they can appear to be proficient readers based on word-reading indicators yet they lack comprehension. Because comprehension is the essence of reading, I need to know if students need help attaining it.	Student self-evaluation, pp. 37–39 Retell and recall, p. 37
How are the student's word recognition skills?	I want to know whether learning English is impacting progress in word recognition.	Miscue analyses with special attention to home language phonology and vocabulary knowledge, pp. 33–37
Do students read with appropriate phrasing, expression, and intonation (e.g., prosody)?	Reading with expression, in meaningful phrases, facilitates comprehension and is a hallmark of proficient readers.	Fluency scale, pp. 38, 40–42

Figure 2–1. The What, Why, and How of Oral Reading Assessment with ELLs

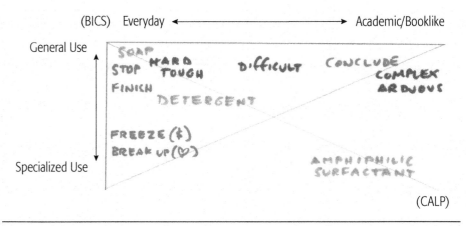

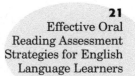

Figure 2–2. Completed Chart for Categorizing Vocabulary Usage

words *religion* and *mysticism* are used in English shows that they are certainly related in meaning, but they are not interchangeable. Students also report to me regularly that the words *soap* and *detergent* have very specific usage in individual households. Some people always say *laundry soap* and others always say *detergent*. Think about what you say at home for what you use to clean dishes. Do you use one word for the dish cleaner you use in the sink, and another for what you put in the dishwasher? It is a safe assumption that only chemists say *amphiphilic surfactant*.

Words with multiple meanings often get placed multiple times in different areas of the chart. In classroom management, for example, many are likely to use words like *act* without realizing that *act* in BICS language might be associated with movies and actors before it is used to talk about group behavior. The word *track* could be categorized as everyday usage if trains or light-rail systems are part of everyday life, but *track* can also be used in more specialized and academic ways (such as a hunting dog tracking an animal, or eyes tracking on a printed page).

While categorizing vocabulary is only one way to take the ELL's perspective, it is nonetheless a significant effort that should result in more appropriate administration and interpretation of assessments. If

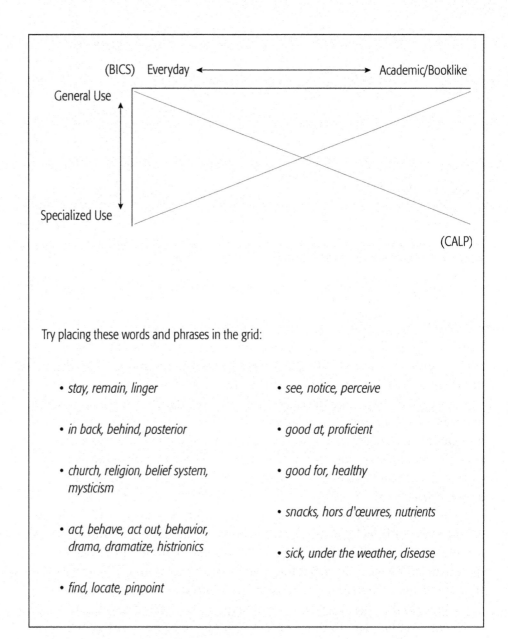

Figure 2–3. Chart for Categorizing Vocabulary Usage

the assessment strategy demands cognitive-academic language, teachers need to be aware of it and adjust accordingly.

Another way to take on the ELL's perspective is to preview and categorize the vocabulary in assessments—especially the words used in comprehension questions. For example, in print there are undoubtedly a variety of discourse marker synonyms: *said* might be replaced by academic equivalents such as *replied*, *cried*, *answered*, *added*, or *declared*. If teachers code these words (with *B* for BICS and *C* for CALP) they will be ready when students may need to hear a synonym in the question, and we can note this adjustment as part of the assessment record. If students need no prompt for a CALP word, teachers can make note of it thereby recording progress in cognitive-academic language.

Principle 2: Safety

As with other children, ELLs may feel an increased sense of risk when they know they are accountable for demonstrating knowledge. So while students may have developed competence, under adverse conditions, their performance may not show it (Chomsky 1965). When students feel risk is high, validity of assessment may be low. It will measure how the student feels more than what she knows. Teachers need to do what they can during assessment to help students feel comfortable and engaged.

One way to ensure that the student feels safe is to provide some scaffolding during informal assessment. While prompting students to attempt what they can without help is important, there are times when an independent response might be too difficult. Providing assistance and recording how students respond sheds light on what students can do *with* help. Many traditional instruments, such as miscue analyses or observation checklists, can easily make room for coding of *independent* and *with help* responses (i.e., unprompted and prompted responses). Simply revise the scoring sheets so that they contain two columns: one for recording success with prompts (synonyms, explanations), and the other for recording unprompted responses. Once tallied, the scores help teachers gain a better sense for the student's zone of proximal development. For example, if a student did not answer a question including the word *declared* but answered when given the word *said*, we now know this student has a foundation for learning the more academic word.

A second way to guarantee safety is to adapt the social environment. Some students need privacy to complete reading assessments, where no other children are monitoring their performance. This is especially true for many of the assessment strategies shown in Figure 2–1. But for ELLs, both privacy *and* the need for a social partner might be warranted. A well-chosen partner might provide just the authentic social support an ELL student desires. If working alone seems stressful, allow the student to invite a partner in.

Principle 3: Appropriate Response

The types of responses ELLs are expected to provide need to be appropriate for their level of language proficiency. Finding ways to leave openings for both simple and complex responses is important. For a student in the starting level, insisting on verbal responses in assessment would be counterproductive. Instead, allowing for *yes/no* head motions or pointing to choices, students still have the option to respond verbally but can choose to respond without the risk of speaking.

Using Observation to Assess Reading

I agree with Peregoy and Boyle (2008) who state that in ELL reading assessment "nothing takes the place of a perceptive and observant teacher, who knows students and watches for their progress throughout the year" (315). Listening and watching ELLs read self-selected books during independent reading and reading conferences provides an understanding of how children perform in a variety of contexts. Consider using questions such as those displayed in Figure 2–4 to guide your observations.

I know! So many questions and so little time! While all of these questions are meant to help, they may instead bring feelings of discomfort if you feel that you must use all of them for every observation. You do not. In fact, I suggest taking one of the questions listed, copying it on a class chart similar to the one in Figure 2–5 and letting that particular question guide your observation for an allotted reading

Observation Question	ELL Considerations
1. Does the student read for meaning?	Among ELLs we frequently find highly motivated word-callers who want to demonstrate proficient word reading for teachers and peers.
2. How well can the child recall or retell what was read?	This is one of the best ways to assess whether an ELL is a word-caller, depending excessively on graphophonic cues as the end purpose of reading.
3. What does the student do when meaning is not maintained?	If ELLs first learn about printed language in grades K–1 when systematic, sequential phonics is taught, they may need additional coaching to know that reading is supposed to be meaningful.
4. Which cues does the child use when unknown word is encountered—syntactic, semantic, and/or graphophonic?	Unlike English-only students, it may be more difficult for ELLs to cue with syntax, which they still may be learning. Student may need extra teaching with this cueing system so they can use it to balance it out against graphophonic cueing.
5. Is there any pattern to the child's miscues?	With ELLs, as with other students, looking for patterns of behaviors across texts adds greater clarity.
6. Does the child depend on teacher or self when difficulties are encountered?	ELLs may depend on the teacher for more and different reasons than English-only students. ELLs may need more scaffolding.
7. Does the student identify high-frequency words?	High-frequency words, especially those that show up on the top fifty in the common lists, are likely to be in ELLs' early oral language vocabulary.
8. Does the reader read with a sense of meaning and expression?	Be aware that the rhythm and meter of other languages are different from U.S. English. In emerging and developing phases, especially, teachers may still hear the patterns of expression from the native language.
9. Is the child willing to talk about the text with another person?	If teachers in the building are fluent in a student's native language, these teachers should be involved in book discussions with ELLs. If only the students or parents who know this language, make every effort, even if across grade levels or inviting parents in, to allow students to talk about books in the home language.
10. How do readers perceive their own reading performance?	Use some of the same smiley face rubrics to check attitude and outlook on reading. Adapt and support students' understanding of the items with visuals, such as pictures of book covers or characters. Also be aware that ELLs may want to appear happy or proficient and that their reported self-perceptions of reading may need to be checked against observations and other data.

Figure 2–4. Suggested Questions and Considerations to Guide Observations of ELL Oral Reading

Date: _____

Question: _____

_____

Student's Name   **Student's Responses**

_____   _____

_____   _____

_____   _____

_____   _____

_____   _____

_____   _____

_____   _____

_____   _____

_____   _____

_____   _____

_____   _____

_____   _____

_____   _____

_____   _____

_____   _____

_____   _____

_____   _____

_____   _____

Figure 2–5. Anecdotal Record

experience. These records can then be stored in notebooks or in file folders and used as evidence for what was observed and as conversations points when talking with students about their progress as language learners and as readers.

Procedures for Assessing Reading in the Starting Stage

Assessing reading can begin in the earliest phases of language acquisition, when listening comprehension is ahead of language production. TESOL levels of language proficiency remind eductors that a learner's silence is typical, and that the child is focused on making sense of linguistic input. In a classroom and in English language texts, language use is highly structured and varied. It takes time for children to figure these things out. This *starting level* lasts about two months. Some children begin producing far earlier than two months, and others take far longer—even a year or more. It really depends on how difficult school is for them to figure out, and how they feel.

When waves of ELL students showed up in U.S. schools in the 1970s–1990s, educators often moved too quickly to identify *starting-stage* ELLs for special education services. The false assumption was that the silence of the starting stage was a sign of disability. Teachers can avoid this fallacy with a few assessment tools to help them learn about ELL reading even before students begin speaking. Keep in mind that *starting-stage assessment questions* are mostly about listening comprehension: What does she understand? When does she understand it? How does she understand? Why does she understand? As students progress upward through language proficiency levels, moving beyond listening comprehension and into reading comprehension is appropriate as is using assessments that require verbal response.

PHYSICAL ASSESSMENT

In the Total Physical Response (TPR) method, assessment is done with the body, rather than with speech. Students stand up when asked to stand, open a book, give a neighbor a high-five, get a pencil from across the room, and otherwise respond without producing language.

This is basically performance-based assessment. When ELLs fail to perform with this type of response, it is often because they did not comprehend what was asked of them. Their actions, or lack thereof, show teachers that they need to make the input more comprehensible by providing physical and social context. Assessment informs instruction, and student performance during instruction is assessment. For teaching reading, book talks surrounding teacher read-alouds can be a context for this kind of assessment.

Among the first resources used should be children's literature texts that can encourage bodily response. Consider the following texts and modify them as appropriate to allow for bodily response.

• Nursery rhymes: *Little Miss Muffet, Humpty Dumpty, Jack and Jill, London Bridge, This Little Pig*

• Songs: "Head, Shoulders, Knees and Toes"; "Five Little Monkeys"

• *We're Going on a Bear Hunt* (M. Rosen and H. Oxenbury 2007). There is also a "Story Play" adaptation of this book by Vivian French. Also check out the YouTube video of Rosen performing the story!

• *Hey Mr. Choo-choo, Where Are You Going?* (Wickberg 2008)

YES/NO AND CHOICE ASSESSMENT

Many books do not make direct demands for students to use their bodies. With these texts, it is up to teachers to give students chances to demonstrate understanding. Consider using one of these two assessment tools: yes/no questions and visual or tactile choice. Figure 2–6 provides sample questions to be used with each. For example, having just read three picture-book versions of "The Three Bears" (an opportunity to use repetition and context to ensure comprehensible input), a teacher might ask a student to respond to the question: "Is the chair broken?" The student can answer with a nod or shake of the head. The picture itself provides context for the question, and we can show either the broken or unbroken chair. This kind of questioning assesses primarily vocabulary understanding, but also involves ELLs authenti-

Yes/No Questions	These questions can demand a head shake or nod, but also encourage simple English responses with the words *yes*, *no*, *is*, *not*, or *isn't*.
Choice Questions	These questions can demand pointing or touching a choice, but also encourage simple English responses such as *this*, *that*, *here*, and *there*. With either/or questions, the answer is in the question.
Open-ended Questions	These questions encourage response involving content words, and elaboration on yes/no and choice responses. Responses can range from single content words to complete sentences. If students do not answer these well, either demand less information or circle back to yes/no and choice questions.

Figure 2–6. Questions for Starting-Stage ELLs (Level 1)

cally in teacher questioning. Instead of giving students an out because they cannot speak, teachers provide them with opportunities to respond and participate at an appropriate level.

Choice responses are equally appropriate. Consider the question: "Is it the small bear or the big bear?" If asking this question while showing a picture with all three bears in it, the child responds by pointing to the picture. Teachers get assessment of vocabulary understanding of *bear* and *small*—if the child points to a bed or something else, teachers gain an idea of her needs. Teachers can ask the same question in a different context, for example, while showing a picture of the small bear and the beds. In this case, we might be focusing on the difference between the words *bed* and *bear*.

This kind of choice work is well supported with picture books, in which illustrations provide context for a valid response. The final page of *Brown Bear, Brown Bear, What Do You See?* (Martin 1970) shows a complete set of characters in review and is perfect for choices. Using manipulatives—such as cut-outs from photocopied book pages—adds additional support. It is easier to arrange a variety of situations when characters and settings are movable (popsicle sticks, magnet tape, flannel board) than it is to flip back and forth between pages. Manipulatives allow for richer student response than mere pointing, because they can be arranged and rearranged to construct a response. For example, when the student is using manipulatives, the teacher can ask, "Which comes first, the large bowl of porridge or the medium bowl? Which comes next? Where does this one go?"

DRAWING AS ASSESSMENT

Drawing is another nonlinguistic medium appropriate for assessing comprehension at a variety of levels. Beyond the simple responses described here, teachers can use drawing to encourage ELLs to show what they understand from larger narrative structures such as events, transitions, problems, solutions, and characters. Responses to literature can give key insight into comprehension. The critical thinking question, "Is Goldilocks a good person or a bad person?" may be better evaluated in drawing than by discussion. I recall one drawing of Goldilocks with a bandit mask on her face. The student obviously understood the story and was working on evaluating character. The visual went much further than simple verbal arguments, because it challenged the story as told by the illustrations not just the words.

INCREASING DEMANDS IN THE STARTING STAGE

As students move between the starting and developing stages, assessments of read-aloud can demand a little more language and/or more understanding. Yes/no questions can be answered verbally with a single word instead of a head motion. They can also be elaborated on. Choices between concrete words (*bears* or *chairs*, *small* or *large*, *eat* or *sit*) can be answered by pointing and gesturing, but also by single word responses such as *this* and *that*. Teachers can ask questions for verbs that give students choices among infinitive forms rather than conjugated forms: "Is she going or staying? Choose *go* or *stay*." If moving into the emerging stage, choice responses can be followed when appropriate by clarification and justification questions: "Why that one? Why not this one?" Simple pointing can be replaced by responses that demand the words *this* and *that*.

Procedures for Assessing Oral Reading
Beyond the Starting Stage

ELLs face challenges that English-only readers do not. When assessing ELLs' reading, teachers need to use their understanding of these challenges to make the assessments valid. For example, English-only readers use their vocabulary knowledge to guide their growth in word-recognition skill. What does the reader do who does not have that depth in English vocabulary? Does she overcompensate with phonics and decoding? Does she use cueing systems that help her maintain meaning?

For ELLs, teachers keep track of reading behaviors they might not mention with English-only readers. For example, they might not keep track of the first time an English-only student says the word *this* when pointing to a picture in a book. But for a starting ELL, saying *this* is a major breakthrough. Using observational checklists is one way to keep track of when readers make transitions that move them across stages.

CIRCUMLOCUTION

For students in the developing and expanding stages, teachers can encourage students' responses by having them use known vocabulary and structures to talk around difficult concepts. This strategy becomes important as soon as students are entering the developing stage. Circumlocution enables teachers to assess understanding without demanding academic or specialized vocabulary and grammar. When students can talk around a concept using everyday words, they are showing that they have a knowledge base sufficient for learning new vocabulary and grammar.

CONTRASTIVE ANALYSIS

Some of the difficulty students experience between home language and English from the developing stage on happens because of systematic linguistic differences, not because of individual knowledge. Swan and Smith (2001) provide *contrastive analysis* for not only sounds but also for grammar and vocabulary between English and twenty-two other languages. When assessing students, remember to be careful about noting miscues or errors related to fluency until you know something about students' home languages. For the languages you see in your school, consider what you can learn from contrastive analysis as an assessment tool.

1. *Vocabulary differences.* Some languages are filled with cognates or sets of words that can be transferred easily from one language to another (e.g., Spanish: *atención, importante, cómico*). Some languages have very few cognates to English, and vocabulary learning is a much more challenging prospect. For students from Quechua-speaking Peru, for example, we expect English vocabulary to be far stranger than for students from Spanish-speaking homes (*escuela = school*) and German homes (*schule = school*).

2. *Grammar and usage differences.* Among the hardest components to learn in a new language is the use of prepositions. *In, at, on, from,* and *for* are particularly difficult. For example, English speakers say "What is on television?" In other languages, the word for *on* is reserved for *on top of* not for things on a wall or other vertical space. When expecting language production from students, teachers should not be surprised during the emerging and developing stages to hear many errors in grammar and usage. During the expanding and bridging stages, teachers might even hear more errors as students try to expand their expressive repertoire.

3. *Written language differences.* While many world languages use a Romanized alphabet, like English, there are other systems. Syllabaries, such as the Japanese kana, are based on symbols that represent common syllables in spoken language. Logograms, as in traditional Chinese writing, can represent entire words or concepts. Many languages use a phonetic alphabet, with the most important sounds represented by letters. But for people from places like Cambodia and Ethiopia, the letters are different looking *and* they behave differently: vowels are found *around* the consonant (above and below, to the left and right). In the Arabic, Hebrew, and Greek alphabets complete vowel markings were not developed until long after the consonant-based alphabet, giving vowel letters an almost secondary role in the writing. Students who know how to read and write in their home language may have significant differences to account for when learning English literacy.

4. *Phonological differences.* Many home languages have sound systems that differ widely from English. What is significant in the home language may not be important in English, and vice versa. For example, Tongan has only six vowel sounds compared to nearly sixteen in English. The slight difference between the English short *e* and short *i* sounds may be almost indistinguishable for a child who is raised speaking and hearing mostly Tongan. When teachers hear articulation errors in reading, they need to understand if articulation errors stem from learning English or from reading difficulty. One of the most basic tools for assessing phonological difference is an International Phonetic Alphabet (IPA) chart. The sound charts of most world languages can be found on Wikipedia, and compared to the sounds of English. A number of online charts will play recordings of the sounds found on an individual language chart, which is helpful for those not common between home language and English. (As examples, check out www.paulmeier.com/ipa/charts.html or www .teachingenglish.org.uk/try/resources/pronunciation/phonemic-chart.)

5. *Cultural and pragmatic differences.* What is appropriate and normal in communication varies from culture to culture. When Udorn showed up in the United States from the Lao refugee camps in Thailand, his teachers made him rather uncomfortable by demanding eye contact. Eye contact with an authority figure in most Southeast Asian cultures is considered an act of defiance, and children in school learn to look downward when responding to a teacher. What do you know about norms for interaction in your students' home cultures? To what extent do your students' families subscribe to these norms? Understanding rather than stereotyping students is the goal.

MODIFIED MISCUE ANALYSIS

Kenneth Goodman's miscue analysis (1969) helps teachers focus on what readers think when they make errors rather than simply counting them. Miscues are not errors because they show that the reader is problem solving like smart readers do. For ELLs, it is even more important to pay attention to the thinking behind a certain kind of miscue, because the thought process might involve language differences inside the typical cueing systems (phonology, syntax, and semantics). As you consider miscue analysis, return to the previous section on home language influence and assess whether, for example, a graphophonic cueing error has its source in differences between English and the home language.

Overuse or underuse of cueing systems can also stem from individual growth in language. For example, the student who knows little academic language may switch primarily to graphophonic cueing when reading a science article in the *Time for Kids* magazine. She knows she can still succeed at decoding words even when she does not understand them.

When we know how ELLs use the cueing systems, we know better how to help them orchestrate all cues to enable easier and more meaningful reading. In Clay's (1979) words, "Teaching can then be likened to a conversation in which you listen to the speaker carefully before you reply."

Here is a version of miscue analysis adapted for classroom use:

1. Choose an appropriate text. Consider the ELL's stage of acquisition first. Although a typical miscue analysis requires 400 words or more, a passage of 150 words may be acceptable for students in the expanding and bridging stages. Consider far shorter passages during the developing stage (25–50 words) and emerging stage (50–100 words). A formal miscue analysis procedure with children in the starting stage may not be very effective.

2. Make copies of Modified Miscue Analysis forms (Figures 2–7 and 2–8).

3. Model the procedure for the ELL. Provide explanation and clarification during the modeling. Be sure to demonstrate clearly that the teacher is listening to the student read out loud and is taking notes.

4. Ask the child to read a passage. Watch her before she begins to read, and during the first phrases. Is she anxious or uncomfortable? Does she remember the most basic things to do: holding the text appropriately, using a finger to point?

Reader's name _____ Grade _____

Title and pages _____ Date _____

Three important questions to ask for each miscue:
M = meaning: Does the miscue make sense?
S = structure: Does the sentence sound right?
V = visual. Does the miscue resemble the printed word?

Student	Text	Cues Used		
		M	S	V
		M	S	V
		M	S	V
		M	S	V
		M	S	V
		M	S	V
		M	S	V
		M	S	V
		M	S	V
		M	S	V
		M	S	V

Figure 2–7. Modified Miscue Analysis Form

1. What did the reader do when unknown words were encountered? (Check all that apply.)

_____ made an attempt in these ways:

___ used meaning cues   ___ used structure cues   ___ used letter-sound cues
___ made repeated tries   ___ used pictures   ___ skipped it and read on
___ used memory   ___ looked at another source
___ other: _____

_____ made no attempt   _____ asked for help   _____ waited for teacher help

2. Which cues did the reader use most often? _____
_____

3. How often did the reader attempt to self-correct when meaning was not maintained?
(Circle one)   always   sometimes   seldom   never
Comments: _____

4. How often did the reader make repetitions? (Circle one)
always   sometimes   seldom   never
Comments: _____

5. Which miscues relate to dialect? _____
Comments: _____

6. Did the reader attend to punctuation?   _____ mostly   _____ somewhat   _____ little
Comments: _____

Comprehension

Retelling was (Circle one):   outstanding   adequate   inadequate
Comments: _____
_____

Other observations:

Figure 2–8. Modified Miscue Analysis Form

5. As the child reads, make the following notations on your copy of the passage:

- Circle words the child omits.
- Insert a carat (^) for words or sounds the child inserts.
- Draw a line through any word that is substituted, and write the substituted word above it.
- Write a *C* on a word the child self-corrects.
- Note repeated words or phrases by writing *R* and drawing a line or arrow back to where the child started repeating.
- Draw slashes (//) between words to show where the child makes phrase breaks.
- If the student makes a miscue that reflects how he usually talks when using English, this is a *language development* issue rather than a reading issue. Note any dialect issues by using a *D* (for dialect).

6. After reading, ask the child to retell what she remembers from the reading. How well does she recall main events from the passage? Would you rate her recall as outstanding, adequate, or inadequate? Can you tell whether the retell shows any understanding or processing, or merely memory?

7. Analyze the child's reading using the Modified Miscue Analysis form (see Figure 2–7).

8. Answer all questions and record additional observations on the Summary of Observations form. Pay special attention to these observations for ELLs. This is where you will account for language-learning impacts on cueing systems.

9. Based on your analysis, determine how you will help the child focus on needed cueing systems, or on how to integrate more than one cueing system.

STUDENT SELF-EVALUATION

When asking ELLs to self-evaluate, remember to make extra effort to give them a frame of reference for what they say. They need to know what they are listening for and how to notice it. It will make sense for

ELLs to be invited to participate with another student in a self-evaluation to learn how it is done. Students and teachers who model this process need to show that candid response, permission to be imperfect, is more important than rating oneself to look good. Modeling self-evaluation of your own readings, including less-effective reading, shows students the importance of honest ratings.

Another way to create a frame of reference for ELLs is to have them reread the same passages or books in recordings, and to compare later readings to earlier ones. The Student Self-Evaluation Form (Figure 2–9) can be used to allow for single readings or comparisons, and with accompanying visuals that provide context for the ratings. The following are suggestions for using the guide:

1. Once a month, ask students to read a passage into a tape recorder. Students listen to their reading and respond to the items on the form.

2. Provide students with time and a private space to complete the reading, listening, and reflection. Pair them up with a partner as necessary for modeling.

3. Ask students to talk to you about their evaluations and why they rated themselves as they did. For ELLs in the emerging to expanding stages, talking about this might be more appropriate than asking for written response.

4. Use the results when designing instruction. For example, does the student notice and describe her own strengths and needs, or does she need help to notice them? Does the student need more attention to be given to creating a meaningful purpose for reading?

FLUENCY SCALE

Oftentimes, fluency is seen as rapid reading and accurate word calling. This is unfortunate for a variety of reasons (Opitz 2007). For ELLs in particular, though, automaticity in word reading can be a misleading indicator of oral reading proficiency as can accuracy. Instead, paying special attention to what sounds appropriate in terms of rhythms of stress and unstressed as they relate to the child's first language is

Student Self-Evaluation

Name _____

Title of Book:

_____

Pages Read: _____

Directions: Write the date in each column for an earlier reading and today's reading. Read each statement. Mark the appropriate pictures.

Statement	Date: / / ← Before		Date: / / After →	
I understood what I read.	☺	😐	☺	😐
I tried to sound like the character.	☺	😐	☺	😐
I read smoothly, like talking to a friend.	☺	😐	☺	😐
I read just right, not too fast, not too slow. Make an X.	🐢 🐇		🐢 🐇	

I knew when I was running into trouble, and here's what I did:

_____

_____

Figure 2–9. Student Self-Evaluation Form

© 2009 Michael F. Opitz and Lindsey Moses, from *Comprehension and English Language Learners*. Portsmouth, NH: Heinemann.

essential. The English language is based on stress rhythms that may not come naturally to speakers of other languages. Thus, when using a fluency scale, teachers need to attend to those elements of fluency that may be impacted by learning a new language while maintaining a different native language.

Let's also remember that comprehension is the essence of reading. As the recent findings of the U.S. Department of Education's findings related to *Reading First* indicate (2008), children made minimal gains in fluency and *they made no gains in reading comprehension*. Clearly, fluency is no guarantee of reading comprehension. So what's a teacher to do when expected to use a fluency scale? I recommend the following procedures:

1. Choose a passage or section of a book. This could be the same reading used for miscue analysis.

2. Make a copy of the passage for each student for making notations. Students read from the original.

3. Read through the Fluency Scale (Figure 2–10). This will orient you to what you are rating.

4. Read the ELL Notes to help you listen for language-learning factors that might impact fluency.

5. Show the passage to a student and allow her to practice reading it silently at least once. Students could also be encouraged to practice until they feel they are ready to be assessed.

6. Ask the student to read the passage orally. During the reading, mark phrasing by placing slashes (//) between the words to show where the student breaks phrases. Write other observations, especially attending to phonology, accent, and rhythm that may come from the student's native language.

7. After reading, ask the student to tell what she remembers from the text. This will provide you with indicators about whether the student was reading for meaning, and help you interpret the type of fluency you hear. It also reminds students that comprehension rules.

Reading Fluency Scale for ELLs

Student's Name: _____

Date: _____

Text Selection:

_____

Directions: Use the scale in all three areas to rate reader fluency. Circle the number in each category that best corresponds to your observations. Observe and note language-learning factors that may impact fluency.

Prosody (phrasing, expression, intonation)

1. Monotone with little sense of phrase boundaries, primarily word-by-word reading
2. Mostly two- and three-word phrases; improper stress and intonation
3. Mixture of phrasing, midsentence pauses for breath, and possibly some choppiness; reasonable stress/intonation
4. Generally well phrased, with adequate attention to expression

ELL Notes

Can you hear rhythm or meter typical of the home language, or a typical accent for ELLs with specific language backgrounds? Do you suspect grammar and usage from native language conflict with English phrases?

Flow

1. Several long pauses, hesitations, sounding out words, repetitions
2. Many extended pauses, hesitations
3. Some breaks in flow, which might be caused by difficulty with specific words and/or structures
4. Reading flows with some breaks, but any word and structure difficulties are resolved quickly, usually through self-correction. Adjusts as necessary to help convey author's intended meaning

ELL Notes

Do you suspect differences in grammar and usage from home language? Do you suspect vocabulary difficulties interrupt the flow?

Reading Rate

1. Slow and arduous
2. Picks up speed a little
3. Uneven mixture of fast and slow reading
4. Consistently conversational. Varies rate to help convey author's intended meaning.

ELL Notes

Listen to student's informal and formal conversational pace for comparison. How does reading pace compare?

Figure 2–10. Sample Fluency Scale with ELL Notes

8. Record your rating in each of the three dimensions of the scale by circling a number (1–4). Make notes in the ELL Notes and on the back of the recording sheet as needed.

9. Attach the marked copy of the passage to the fluency scale sheet.

10. Interpret the results and design instruction accordingly.

TIMED READING

Timed measures appear to be the norm in the new millennium. Debates about their value aside, of interest here is that they commonly make unfair demands on ELLs to perform a benchmark number of correct items in a given time frame. As with many children, ELLs often simply need more time to read and to process information. This is especially true for comprehension indicators such as retelling, answering questions, and summarizing. Modifying the time limit for ELLs is anything but a choice if the goal is for them to truly under-stand what it is they know and need to know in order to advance as readers of English. The Center for Applied Linguistics provides analy-ses of norm-referenced assessment instruments, showing whether they include norms for ELLs (usually Spanish, www.cal.org/twi/assessments.pdf.)

So there you have them: some reasonable and effective ways to use oral reading to assess ELLs. To be sure, some take more time than others to administer, score and interpret, yet all are manageable. When making decisions about selecting assessment strategies, staying focused on the purpose for the assessment and how the results will be used to inform instruction is essential.

Using Oral Reading with Starting Language Learners (Level 1)

It was Hannah's first day in a classroom where I (Lindsey) was conducting research; she just moved from the Netherlands and did not speak any English. In the late morning, I noticed her doing the "potty dance" and asked her if she needed to go to the bathroom. She looked panicked, but didn't seem to understand what I had said. I put my hand out, she grabbed it, and I walked her down to the bathroom. She looked excited, started nodding her head up and down, and ran into the bathroom. When we got back to class, I made her a little card that with the word bathroom *and a drawing of the women's sign found outside public restrooms. I walked her back to the bathroom, showed her the card, and said "Bathroom." She nodded, so I said it again while I pointed at the word* bathroom *and then pointed to the bathroom. I gave her the card to signal when she needed to go to the bathroom without having to communicate verbally.*

Students in the *starting level*, like Hannah, often do not speak in English and typically respond using nonverbal cues such as gesturing or pointing to communicate basic needs or respond to others. This use of nonverbal cues shows evidence that they are developing a listening vocabulary and are comprehending. Clearly, students in this starting stage of language acquisition understand much more than they can articulate.

Understanding the characteristics of students in level 1, teachers are better able to provide appropriate and nonthreatening instruction. This instruction includes, but is not limited to, modeling oral reading, allowing more advanced students to model oral reading, providing repeated exposure to texts, and giving students opportunities to participate in group activities in which they won't be singled out. Using gestures, puppets, environmental print, and wordless picture books, teachers provide comprehensible input to help students gain access to print.

Figure 3–1 is an overview of appropriate oral reading strategies that teachers can use when designing instruction focused on helping students at this starting level to better understand how to read English. Regardless of the activity, one underlying premise ties them together: *students only speak when they are ready!*

Reading Skills	Say It with the Puppet	Sing a Song	Read the Pictures	Teacher Read-Aloud	Read Your World
Positive Attitudes/Interest in Reading	•	•	•	•	•
Reading Comprehension			•		•
Listening Comprehension	•	•		•	
Social Vocabulary	•	•	•		•
Academic Vocabulary		•	•	•	•
Use of Language Cues			•		•
Predicting			•	•	
Forming Images	•	•	•	•	
Using Prior Knowledge			•	•	•
Monitoring			•		
Inferring	•		•	•	
Fluency (R = rate, A = accuracy, P = prosody)	P	P		R A P	A
Skimming					

Figure 3–1. Effective Oral Reading Strategies and Skills for Starting Language Learners

Say It with the Puppet

Instructional Information

Puppets provide a safe environment for ELLs who feel uncomfortable talking face to face. Krashen (1982) emphasizes the importance of this safe environment when explaining his affective filter hypothesis of acquiring and learning a language. According to Krashen, when the classroom atmosphere is relaxed, the affective filter is low, which enables children to be more receptive to input resulting in accelerated language acquisition. Using puppets is one way to create this relaxed atmosphere because puppets take the focus off of students allowing them to talk to others with much greater ease. Talking enables students to further enhance conversational English (BICS) and creates an opportunity to further develop listening comprehension. When children watch a puppet play, for instance, they need to stay focused on the meaning rather than how the puppet is articulating words to more fully engage in the show.

Savvy Suggestions

1. Select a whole text or a text passage to read aloud. The text should contain a simple story line with easily identifiable characters. Enlarge the text for all to see.

2. Read the text aloud. Once finished, use oral language prompts to encourage students to talk about the text. Appropriate prompts for emerging ELLs include, "Show me . . . ," "Which of these . . .?", "Point to . . . ," and "Is this a . . . ?"

3. Introduce the puppets that coincide with the story. Model how to use the puppets to act out the text.

4. Provide guided practice by having students join you with puppets for the other characters to model for the class. Read through the text and practice using the puppets with different students multiple times.

5. Put the text and the puppets in a center for literacy time. Small groups of students can practice reading, summarizing, and/or silently using puppets to reenact the story.

77

7## Classroom Conversations

Recognizing that some of his second-grade ELLs were at the starting level, Tom decides to use puppetry as one way of helping students acquire and use conversational English. Today he has selected *Finklehopper Frog* (Livingston 2003) because the book has two primary characters who talk with one another. Both characters convey acceptance of one another's differences and help the other minor characters in the book to do the same. Tom begins by reading the book aloud to the students. When he is finished reading, he invites students' comments saying, "So what did you think of the story?" Once students have had an opportunity to volunteer their ideas, Tom then takes them back through the book and uses specific oral language prompts to encourage their talking. Turning to page 1, he says, "Show me Finklehopper Frog." Turning to page 2, he comments, "Which of these is Finklehopper?" He proceeds through the book in like manner. Once finished with the review, Tom pulls out the puppets he has brought that go with the story. Using the frog puppet, he models how to use it to say something that Finklehopper said. He then tries on the rabbit puppet and does the same. Once he has modeled for the students, he suggests that they give it a try. After students have had this time to practice using the puppets, Tom closes the lesson saying, "Puppets can help us to understand what we have read. They can also help us to talk with one another. I'm going to put the book and the puppets in the puppet theatre center so that you can use them during center time."

Terrific Texts for *Say It with the Puppet*

Title	Author (Last, First)	Publisher/Year	ISBN
Ping Pong Pig	Church, Caroline	Holiday House/2008	9780823421763
Say Hello	Foreman, Jack Foreman, Michael	Candlewick/2008	9780763636579

Title	Author (Last, First)	Publisher/Year	ISBN
Five Little Firefighters	Graham, Tom	Henry Holt & Company/2008	9780805086973
Finklehopper Frog	Livingston, Irene	Tricycle/2003	9781582460758
Little Panda	Liwska, Renata	Houghton Mifflin/2008	9780618966271
Peter and the Wolf	Raschka, Chris	Atheneum/2008	9780689856525
Little Hoot	Rosenthal, Amy	Chronicle/2008	9780811860239
Melvin Might?	Scieszka, Jon	Simon & Schuster/2008	9781847385079
Hello World! Greetings in 42 Languages Around the Globe!	Stojic, Manya	Cartwheel Books/2002	9780439362023
Blue Goose	Tafuri, Nancy	Simon & Schuster/2008	9781416928348

Winning Websites

www.puppetools.com provides a wealth of resources for creating and purchasing puppets as well as ideas for how to use them.

www.puppet.org provides information about the Center for Puppetry and its many resources for teachers and parents alike.

www.puppetryinpractice.com provides several ideas for how puppetry can be used to teach the arts. This particular site offers information about the value of using puppetry with ELLs.

Handy Hints

Puppets can be used in many content areas. Children can use them to reenact something they have been reading in social studies. For example, children in upper elementary grades might create a puppet of a president or another historical figure and use the puppet to tell information about the given individual.

Sing a Song

Instructional Information

Singing songs is a positive way to assist students in second language acquisition and ELLs' literacy development (Peregoy and Boyle 2008). Suzanne Medina (2002) highlights how songs can help ELLs acquire vocabulary and grammar knowledge and improve spelling and linguistic skills of reading, writing, speaking, and listening. Incorporating motions with the songs can make the singing and learning more entertaining and meaningful (Ohman-Rodriguez 2004; Saricoban and Metin 2000) while providing comprehensible input for new vocabulary words.

Using music is an enjoyable and nonthreatening activity for most students, and it provides a practice in which repetition is expected and needed for all students regardless of their language proficiency. Therefore, it doesn't isolate ELLs as the only students who require multiple exposures to the text/song. The songs provide students with authentic examples of English while also targeting vocabulary, grammar, listening comprehension, and oral reading in a relaxed environment, weakening the affective filter (Krashen 1982) and optimizing learning.

Savvy Suggestions

1. Select an age-appropriate musical passage to read and sing aloud.

2. Write the lyrics (text) on a chart or overhead transparency using one color to highlight specific vocabulary and another color to underline the chorus or repetitive portion of the song.

3. Model singing the song or play the song using an accompanying CD (if provided) as you point to the lyrics on the chart or overhead transparency with the pointer.

4. Once students have heard the song for enjoyment, review the vocabulary and repetitive portions pointing to each as you read them aloud.

5. To show understanding of the vocabulary, have volunteers act out words or refrains.

6. Repeat the song again, inviting students to join you as they feel comfortable. Continue to use the pointer to highlight the specific vocabulary and repeated refrains.

7. Continue practicing throughout the week and invite student volunteers to do the pointing.

8. Place the text in the reading center for children to use during independent reading.

Classroom Conversations

Understanding that music is a vehicle to help emerging language learners causes Rachel to use songs. Today she selected *Don't Laugh at Me* (Seskin and Shamblin 2002) because the song directly ties into some of the bullying problems that she is seeing on the playground. She begins by playing the song to the children while pointing to the lyrics on the chart. She then revisits repetitive lyrics, "Don't laugh at me. Don't call me names. Don't get your pleasure from my pain." She points out the words *don't laugh,* and *me*. As she points to each word, she shows the student an action to represent that word: for *don't*, she shakes her finger and head side-to-side; for *laugh*, she puts her head back and laughs; for *me*, she points to herself. When she is finished, she reviews the vocabulary and asks student to do the action with her for each vocabulary word. The song is played during the next reading, and she again reviews the vocabulary. She then asks for their reflections saying, "Try to show me how the people in this song might feel when they are laughed at or called names." Once students have shared their responses, she plays the song again while using a pointer to point to the lyrics on the overhead and asks students to join in as they feel comfortable. She provides students daily practice throughout the week. She then places the familiar text and chart in the reading center to use during independent reading time.

Terrific Texts for *Sing a Song*

Title	Author (Last, First)	Publisher/Year	ISBN
Norman Rockwell: You're a Grand Old Flag	Cohan, George	Atheneum/2008	9781416917700
Ralph's World Rocks!	Covert, Ralph	Henry Holt & Company/2008	9780805087352
Forever Young	Dylan, Bob	Ginee Seo Books/2008	9781416958086
She'll Be Coming 'Round the Mountain	Emmett, Jonathan	Simon & Schuster/2006	9781416936527
I Got Two Dogs	Lithgow, John	Simon & Schuster/2008	9781416958819
We're Going on a Leaf Hunt	Metzger, Steve	Scholastic/2005	9780439873772
Hush, Little Baby	Pinkney, Brian	Greenwillow/2006	9780060559946
Don't Laugh at Me	Seskin, Steve Shamblin, Allen	Tricycle/2002	9781582460581
There Was a Wee Woman	Silverman, Erica	Melanie Kroupa Books/2008	9780374382537
Where Is Home, Little Pip?	Wilson, Karma	Margaret K. McElderry Books/2008	9780689859830

Winning Websites

www.songsforteaching.com/esleflesol.html provides songs for teaching grammar and conversational English (BICS).

www.forefrontpublishers.com/eslmusic has lesson plans, materials that have been helpful for using music for second language instructional purposes, articles supporting music and ESL, books and tapes, and other web links.

www.funsongs.co.uk provides sample downloads for original action song packages using Total Physical Response (TPR) and tips about using action songs.

Handy Hints

1. Songs like "Row, Row, Row, Your Boat" and "Mary Had a Little Lamb" can be used to teach and reinforce pronunciation of consonant sounds, and songs like "Old MacDonald Had a Farm," "BINGO," and "The Alphabet Song" can be used to introduce and teach individual letter sounds or spelling.

2. At all grade levels, teachers can use a familiar tune like "Twinkle, Twinkle Little Star" to teach new concepts, spelling, or vocabulary by creating their own lyrics to a familiar melody. For example, a teacher who wants to reinforce the new vocabulary or concepts learned about a desert habitat might write something like the following (to the tune of "Twinkle, Twinkle Little Star"):

   Desert, desert hot and dry
   Rain rarely falls from the sky.
   Lizards and snakes both live here
   Cacti and sand are always near
   Desert, desert hot and dry
   Rain rarely falls from the sky.

Read the Pictures

Instructional Information

Illustrations provide a common language for children of all linguistic backgrounds. For this reason, wordless picture books are an aesthetically pleasing way to engage ELLs in the starting level. Margaret Early (1991) discusses how wordless picture books can be used with ELLs to enhance both oral language and literacy development across a variety of text types, topics, and thinking skills. These books can be used to contextualize the language in meaningful ways as both the teacher and other students tell a story to accompany the illustrations. The storytelling contextualized with illustrations enables students to further develop their listening comprehension and conversational English (BICS). Allowing the ELLs to join in the storytelling of the wordless picture books provides them with a nonthreatening opportunity to begin using acquired vocabulary and conversational English (BICS) so that the teacher and other students can understand the meaning behind the linguistic appropriations without having to question the learner.

Savvy Suggestions

1. Select a wordless picture book.

2. Model taking a two-minute picture walk through the text. Draw attention to the fact that the book does not contain any words.

3. Go back to the first page of the text and tell the students what you think is happening in the picture. Model this as a storytelling of the pictures for a couple of pages.

4. Provide guided practice by having the students suggest an idea of what is happening in the picture to a partner before sharing aloud one of their ideas to the class.

5. Use ideas from students to complete a class story of the wordless picture book.

6. Provide students with time to create their own stories of wordless picture books in small groups or with a partner.

Classroom Conversations

Bryan decides to use a wordless picture book in his classroom as a way of helping his ELLs in the starting level develop their oral language and vocabulary development. Today he selected *Wave* (Lee 2008) because it includes a main character, a young girl, at the beach chasing and playing in the ocean waves. The plot line is simple, easy to follow, and includes vocabulary that could be easily identified by students in the emerging stage. Bryan models taking a picture walk and asks the students what they notice about this book that is different from other books they have seen. A student points out that the book does not contain any words. Bryan agrees and tells the students that he and the class will make up a story to accompany the illustrations. He starts by turning to the first page and says, "A little girl named Suzy went to the beach with her mom. She ran toward the ocean." He continues with this until he gets to page 7. Then, he asks the students to turn and share what they would say on this page. He provides a language frame by saying, "The little girl, Suzy, is. . . ." After giving the students time to share with their partners, he asks for volunteers to share their idea with the class. Stephen volunteers, "The little girl, Suzy, is sitting and looking at the wave." Bryan points at the girl and makes a motion with his finger pointing at how she is sitting while he repeats, "The little girl, Suzy, is sitting." Then he points from her eyes to the wave while he repeats, "and looking at the wave." Bryan continues to give guidance with succeeding pages throughout the remainder of the book. Bryan closes the lesson by saying, "Now that you've had practice with this book, when you meet with me in your small group today, we're going to use this book again to create and listen to stories. I will also put other wordless picture books in the reading center so that you can practice creating, telling, and listening to different stories."

Terrific Texts for *Read the Pictures*

Title	Author (Last, First)	Publisher/Year	ISBN
Stick	Breen, Steve	Dial/2007	9780803731240
Carl's Summer Vacation	Day, Alexandra	Farrar, Straus & Giroux/2008	9780374310851
Polo: The Runaway Book	Faller, Regis	Roaring Brook Press/2007	9781596431898
Colors Everywhere	Hoban, Tana	Greenwillow/1995	9780688127626
Wave	Lee, Suzy	Chronicle/2008	9780811859240
Trainstop	Lehman, Barbara	Houghton Mifflin/2008	9780618756407
Wonder Bear	Nyeu, Tao	Dial/2008	9780803733282
Fun with Hieroglyphs	Roehrig, Catharine	Metropolitan Museum of Art and Simon & Schuster/2008	9780670835768
Flotsam	Wiesner, David	Houghton Mifflin/2006	9781428702066
The Little Red Fish	Yoo, Tae-Eun	Penguin/2007	9780803731455

Winning Websites

http://nancykeane.com/rl/317.htm provides a list of wordless picture books.

www.library.uiuc.edu/edx/wordless.htm provides bibliographies of wordless picture books organized by teaching category and topic.

www.readwritethink.org/lessons/lesson_view.asp?id=130 has lesson plans for using wordless picture books with ELLs.

Handy Hints

A great deal of strategies that promote reading skills with content texts can be altered and used with wordless picture books. Options for *before reading* include, but are not limited to, introducing and previewing new vocabulary using the text illustrations or Robinson's (1946) SQ3R, having students *survey, question, read, recite,* and *review. During reading*, the teacher can scribe as the class creates a story to accompany the illustrations, or more advanced students could write their own stories. *After-reading* activities could include telling the story to friends or partners, writing and publishing individual or classroom texts to accompany the illustrations, or creating their own wordless picture book.

Teacher Read-Aloud

Instructional Information

Reading aloud to children is perhaps one of the best ways to help children become competent language users. In fact, the findings of numerous researchers investigating the power of the read-aloud have led them to report that reading aloud to children boosts their listening vocabularies (Elley 1989), their ability to use spoken English (Cohen 1968), phonological awareness (Nuemann 1999; Ayers 1993), acquisition of vocabulary (Ulanoff and Pucci 1999), and reading comprehension (Dickinson and Smith 1994). These findings, coupled with the enjoyment factor that accompanies reading aloud to children, are all sound reasons for making the read-aloud an integral part of the language arts curriculum. Especially as it pertains to ELLs, the teacher read-aloud can help children hear how informal conversational English (BICS) differs from the more formal English (CALP) that authors use to construct books.

Reading aloud to children involves much more than simply pulling any book off of the shelf, sitting the children on the floor, and reading. Instead, teachers select specific books for specific reasons. For example, at times they will focus on selecting texts that will expose children to the different text structures authors use when constructing texts. Having these structures implanted in their minds through listening better enables children to feel more at ease when they encounter these same structures when reading different texts on their own. At other times, teachers will focus on teaching children print conventions such as left-to-right progression and speech-to-print match. At still other times, the teacher might want to demonstrate how fluent reading sounds. Just as important, however, is the enjoyment factor! Reading aloud provides an opportunity for teachers to show children how much they enjoy reading.

Savvy Suggestions

Preparing for the Read-Aloud

1. Choose a text that is at the students' attention, interest, and concept-development levels. Make sure that you enjoy the text, too.

2. Practice reading the text so that you are comfortable with it and so that you know just how you want to read it to students.

3. Designate a time and inviting place in the classroom for the read-aloud experience. Some teachers like to have a comfortable upholstered chair to sit on while reading to children who are seated in front of them on a carpet. Others like to provide a cozy environment by using floor lamps and floor pillows.

During the Read-Aloud

1. Call children to the read-aloud area and give them some time to get seated and positioned so that they can see the text.

2. State the title of the book and show the text to the children. Provide time for children to make some predictions about what they might expect to hear.

3. Tell them to listen for given teaching points.

4. Read the text to the students.

5. Stop at key points and have them predict what might happen or have them state the refrain of the story (if there is one).

6. State more questions for the students to think about while they are listening to the story.

After the Read-Aloud

Have students answer some of the unanswered questions and do one or more of the following based on your purpose for doing the read-aloud: talk about the text they have just heard, retell significant parts, dramatize it, or construct another ending. You might also want to call attention to the way you read the story and ask students why you slowed down or read some parts more quickly and expressively than other parts of the story. Finally, if you want to reflect on your read-aloud performance, you might find the form shown in Figure 3–2 helpful.

Classroom Conversations

Roland reads to his third graders at least once a day because he enjoys the positive feelings that emanate among all during it. Enjoyment front and center, he has other reasons for making the read-aloud a regularly recurring event and for selecting specific texts for any given read-aloud. Today he has selected *Little Mama Forgets* (Cruise 2006) because it contains several Spanish words and phrases embedded throughout the story. Recognizing that some of his third graders are Spanish speakers who at the *starting level* in terms of learning English, he feels that this will be a perfect book to help them use what they know about Spanish and better understand the English text. He begins the read-aloud by doing a two-minute picture walk, pointing to some of the Spanish phrases. After this warm-up, he tells students, "Now that you are a little familiar with the book, I'll read it to you. Listen for the Spanish words and see if you can figure out what they mean when used with the English words." He then reads the story aloud as students listen. Once finished, Roland simply sits and pauses to provide time for any volunteers to respond. Orlando breaks the silence saying, "I liked the story. It reminds me of me and my mama." Other students chime in with their favorite parts. Once their talking subsides, Roland calls attention to the Spanish words and phrases by turning to specific pages on which they appear. Remembering that he has several children who are *starting English language learners*, he uses specific questioning techniques such as, "Point to . . ." that will ensure their success. "Point to the phrase that says *Buenos dias*," he asks. Once a student points, he then asks, "What does that mean in this story?" He continues like this until all Spanish words and phrases have been discussed. He closes the lesson by saying, "Reading can be a lot of fun. And understanding what you read is part of the fun. Using what you know about some words is one way to learn about new words. I'll leave this book in the reading center so that you can reread it during independent silent reading time if you so choose."

To what degree did I . . .	Little	Some	A lot
1. familiarize myself with the text before sharing it with students?			
2. relax and speak loud enough for all to hear?			
3. alter my phrasing by attending to punctuation and the emotion it was intended to convey?			
4. change the pace of my reading to reflect the story action?			
5. read with emotion?			
6. hold the book so that all could see?			
7. pause when I finished to give listeners time to think about the text and time to offer their thoughts?			

Figure 3–2. Teacher Read-Aloud Self-Assessment

Terrific Texts for *Teacher Read-Aloud*

Title	Author (Last, First)	Publisher/Year	ISBN
Little Mama Forgets	Cruise, Robin	Melanie Kroupa Books/ 2006	9780374346133
Super Oscar	De La Hoya, Oscar Shulman, Mark	Simon & Schuster/2006	9781416906117
Mary Engelbreit's Mother Goose Favorites	Engelbreit, Mary	HarperCollins/2008	9780061575440
Don't Worry Bear	Foley, Greg	Viking/2008	9780670062454
Say Hello	Foreman, Jack	Candlewick/2008	9780763636576
Corduroy 40th Anniversary Edition	Freeman, Don	Viking/2008	9780670063369
Miss Smith Reads Again!	Garland, Michael	Dutton/2006	9780525477228
What a Family!	Isadora, Rachel	G. P. Putnam's Sons/2006	9780399242540
Can Anybody Hear Me?	Meserve, Jessica	Clarion Books/2008	9780547028347
Ducks Don't Wear Socks	Nedwidek, John	Viking/2008	9780670061365
Houdini the Amazing Caterpillar	Pederson, Janet	Clarion Books/2008	9780618893324

Winning Websites

www.rif.org contains several books for children to follow along as they are read aloud.

www.ala.org provides several lists of books suitable for read-alouds.

www.readquarium.com provides a wealth of books that are read aloud online.

Handy Hints

1. While some books may be read cover to cover, not all books need to be. You might choose to read a section of a book to either make the text more manageable for *starting language learners* or as an incentive for children to read the remainder of the text independently.

2. When using a book that has a repetitive refrain, consider inviting the students to join in with the reading as they feel comfortable.

Read Your World

Instructional Information

Read Your World is all about capitalizing on environmental print as a way of helping children see that they already know how to read some English words thus igniting their desire to further learn how to read a variety of texts. In the words of Orellana and Hernandez (1999), "By linking the reading of *words* to the reading of *worlds* that children know best, we can spark their enthusiasm for literacy learning in school" (619).

Harris and Hodges (1995) define environmental print as "print and other graphic symbols, in addition to books, that are found in the physical environment, [such] as street signs, billboards, television commercials, building signs" (73). And, as several researchers have noted, it is print that children read before they ever encounter words in books (Harste, Burke, and Woodward 1982). Researchers also note that using environmental print to teach reading is advantageous because doing so builds on what children already know about how print functions, provides a "cognitive anchor" for connecting sounds with printed symbols, provides easy access to print, and engenders feelings of success because text appears in manageable chunks (Kuby 1999, 2004; Kennedy 2001). Likewise, using environmental print as one part of a reading program helps children to expand their notion of what it means to be a reader. Right from the start children see that readers read all kinds of texts both in and out of school.

Savvy Suggestions

1. Provide some sort of experience that includes the reading of environmental print. This might be as simple as bringing in a variety of food containers and sharing them with students or taking them on a neighborhood walk, a school tour, or a field trip to a local grocery store. In any case, talk with students about the print they see.

2. Tell students that what they are reading is print that is in their environment and that they can recognize it because of the colors or shapes that go with the print.

3. Read aloud a text that coincides with the particular experience you provided. If you went on a neighborhood walk, for example, you might read aloud *I Read Signs!* (Hoban 1987).

4. As you read the book, point out the signs that are similar to those you saw on your walk.

5. Emphasize to students that reading words in their world is one form of reading and that many times these same words are found in books.

Classroom Conversations

Michael uses environmental print to help his first graders, many of whom are *starting ELLs*, learn that what they see in their world is also what authors use to create books. He decides to take them on a neighborhood walk and points out the signs along the way, all the while asking for students to tell what they see. When coming to a stop sign, for example, he stops, points to it and asks, "Who knows that this sign says?" Few students hold back stating, "Stop!" Michael then says, "You are correct, but how do you know?" and gives students time to share their ideas. Kayla notes, "I know it says *stop* because the sign is red." Marcelo notes, "I know it says *stop* because it has a funny shape." Yet another student comments, "It starts with an *s*. That's how I know it says *stop*." Michael then states, "You are all correct! Sometimes when we read the print in our environment, we use the color, shape, and the letters on the sign to read it and to understand what the sign is telling us to do." He continues like this as they take their neighborhood walk.

Once back in the classroom, Michael gathers the students in the reading area and reads aloud *I Read Signs!* (Hoban 1987). He prepares them by stating, "Now that you have had some time to take a look at the signs in your environment, let's take a look at this book and see if this author uses the same signs in the book. I'll read the sign shown on the page. If the sign is like the one we saw on our walk, point your thumb up. If it is not, point your thumb down. If you can't remember, point your thumb sideways." He then proceeds to read the book. Once finished, he gives students time to think about the book. One student says, "Let's read it again!" Taking his cue from this student, Michael says, "OK, but this time, let's keep count of how many signs are like those we saw and those we did not see when we took our walk. We'll use this chart. I'll need a recorder." He then displays a chart that shows two columns, *Signs We Saw/Signs We Did Not See* and appoints a volunteer to place a tally mark in the correct column after rereading each sign in the book. He closes the lesson by saying, "So you can see that authors sometimes use the very same print in their books that we see in our world. They help us to see that we can use many different kinds of texts for reading."

Terrific Texts for *Read Your World*

Title	Author (Last, First)	Publisher/Year	ISBN
Signs in Our World	DK Publishing	DK Children/2006	9780756618346
Signs at the Park	Hill, Mary	Children's Press/2003	9780516243658
Signs at School	Hill, Mary	Children's Press/2003	9780516243665
Signs at the Store	Hill, Mary	Children's Press/2003	9780516743634
I Read Symbols!	Hoban, Tana	Greenwillow/1983	9780688023324
I Read Signs!	Hoban, Tana	HarperTrophy/1987	9780688073312
ABC Drive!	Howland, Naomi	Clarion/1994	9780395664148
Grocery Store	Leeper, Angela	Heinemann Raintree/2004	9781403451699
City Signs	Milich, Zoran	Kids Can Press/2008	9781553377481
Alphabet City	Pelletier, David	Puffin/1999	9780140559040

Winning Websites

www.hubbardscupboard.org/i_can_read_.html offers a wealth of colorful logos of specific products that you can download. This site also offers several teaching suggestions.

www.thesolutionsite.com/lpnew/lesson/11903/overview.html offers five specific lessons that incorporate environmental print.

www.readwritethink.org provides several lessons for using environmental print including *Stop Signs, McDonald's, and Cheerios: Writing with Environmental Print* and *I Know That Word! Teaching Reading with Environmental Print.*

Handy Hints

Environmental print can be used in many ways to teach many skills. For example, children can use various labels and logos for word-sorting activities. They can sort the labels according to beginning sounds, those that are found in school/out of school, or any other myriad of categories. These same labels can be used to create or add to the existing word wall. If a word wall already exists, for example, students can add labels to the appropriate section (e.g., corresponding letter of the alphabet). Food labels and signs can also be compiled into student- or classmade books that become part of the classroom library. Children can then read these books during independent silent reading time.

Using Oral Reading with Emerging Language Learners (Level 2)

The first day back from winter break, I (Lindsey) read the prompt I had printed on the whiteboard to my second graders, finishing it by stating one thing I had done over the winter break. I then asked them to do the same. I commented, "Let's read this sentence together. You read and I'll point to the words." As I pointed to the words, the class chorally read, "One thing I did during break was _____." "So what did you do?" I asked. "Think of one activity and share it with your neighbor. Remember to start by saying the prompt on the board." After the talking had subsided, I asked for volunteers to share with the whole group. Will, a native English speaker, said, "One thing I did during break was go to a movie." Jorge, a native Spanish speaker, commented, "One thing I did during break was look at TV." After a few volunteers had shared, I then asked the students to write a journal entry using the same prompt they had used to start their oral speaking. Jorge turned to Will and requested, "Pencil please." After Will gave him a pencil, Jorge replied, "Thank you" and began writing. In his journal entry he wrote, "One thing I did during break was luk et tv."

Teachers like Lindsey know that students in the *emerging level* are starting to understand many phrases and simple sentences. They can communicate using groups of words and memorized phrases for basic social interactions, routine situations, and when basic needs need to be met. Just like Jorge, learners at this stage can use selected simple structures correctly, but continue to produce some errors in speech and writing. As they begin to use general academic vocabulary and common expressions, they demonstrate their English acquisition development as they move from the *starting level* to the *emerging level.*

Understanding and recognizing the characteristics of ELLs in the *emerging level* enables teachers to provide meaningful and appropriate instruction. At this stage, it is beneficial to use effective oral reading strategies to model proficient reading and to provide the safe environment learners need in order to participate. Strategies such as *Shared Reading, Fill the Gaps,* and *Chime Right In* provide nonthreatening, scaffolded learning opportunities for English language production. Figure 4–1 is an overview of oral reading strategies that teachers can use when designing instruction focused on helping students at this *emerging level* better understand how to read English.

Strategies

Reading Skills	Shared Reading	Fill the Gaps	Draw, Tell, and Listen	Think-Aloud, Think Along, Think Alone	Chime Right In
Positive Attitudes/Interest in Reading	•	•	•	•	•
Reading Comprehension	•	•		•	•
Listening Comprehension			•	•	•
Social Vocabulary			•	•	•
Academic Vocabulary	•	•		•	•
Use of Language Cues	•	•		•	•
Predicting		•		•	
Forming Images			•		
Using Prior Knowledge			•	•	•
Monitoring	•	•		•	
Inferring		•		•	
Fluency (R = rate, A = accuracy, P = prosody)	R A P	A			P
Skimming					

Figure 4–1. Effective Oral Reading Strategies and Skills for Emerging Language Learners

Shared Reading

Instructional Information

Donald Holdaway conceived the idea of *shared reading* (i.e., *Shared Book Experience* or *SBE*) in 1979 as a way to engage the ELLs he was teaching in Australia. In addition to emphasizing that the reading experience needed to be enjoyable, interesting, and relaxed, Holdaway also emphasized that shared reading was a way to expose children to good literature and students' socialization simultaneously. He emphasized that the experience should emulate the nonthreatening reading experience a child might have at home. Thirty years later, we have some evidence that it is an effective way to increase students' ability to analyze words, both literal and inferential comprehension, writing, and grammar (Reutzel, Hollingsworth, and Eldredge 1994; Elley and Mangubhai 1983). Elley's findings in particular (Elley 1989, 1991) point to the success of shared reading as a way of boosting ELLs' reading ability.

Given that students at the *emerging level* can communicate by using memorized phrases and groups of words, shared reading is an appropriate way to engage them. That is, many of the books used for shared reading encourage students to memorize and use repetitive phrases and groups of words. Students are seated in front of an enlarged text (i.e., big book) written with supportive language elements such as rhyme, rhythm, and repetition. Elements such as these make the book predictable (Opitz 1995). After a focused introduction and a first read by the teacher, students chime in on a second reading. Students are afforded with numerous opportunities to develop both BICS (as a result of talking with one another about story events) and CALP (by hearing and reading a story that uses academic vocabulary). Students learn about language by using it to accomplish specific purposes.

Savvy Suggestions *(based on Holdaway 1979)*

1. Choose a big book that meets the needs of the group. What's most important here is to choose a book that showcases specific language features such as rhyme, rhythm, and repetition. The book must be large enough for all to see. Sometimes books are manufactured specifically as big books. Or, you can enlarge the text using overhead transparencies of the text or an Elmo projector.

2. Set a purpose for the shared reading.

3. Introduce the book by pointing to and reading the title, author's name, and illustrator's name. You may briefly introduce a character or a small portion of the events that will allow the students to connect with and anticipate the story. Provide time for students to predict what the book might be about.

4. Read the text aloud to the students. Point to the words as they are read in order to demonstrate that the written words convey meaning.

5. Read the text again and stop occasionally to point out how your manner of reading changes according to the meaning of the text (i.e., dialogue or rising action).

6. Reread the text several times over several days. Invite students to read along, as they feel comfortable. As students become more proficient with the text, allow individual students to read and designate a text pointer.

7. Encourage students to talk about the story (e.g., likes, dislikes, funny parts, connections).

8. Place the book in the reading center so that students can reread it during independent reading time.

Classroom Conversations

Josh wants to help all of his kindergarteners understand that words are often associated with specific content. He realizes that this work helps all students, including *emerging level ELLs*, learn some academic vocabulary. Following the previously listed procedures, Josh gathers students in the reading area to share *Hey Mr. Choo-choo, Where Are You Going?* (Wickberg 2008). He opens the lesson by talking with students. He comments, "Tell me what you know about trains." Students have no difficulty sharing their ideas. Miguel takes the lead, "The train that goes by my house is very loud!" Julie chimes in, "I got to ride a train. There was a funny looking man telling us to get on the train." As they share, Josh writes some of their ideas on the chart paper he has displayed. He then comments, "Wow! You know a lot about trains! Today we're going to read a book that tells you even more." He shows them the cover of the book and states, "This particular author is trying to help you to better understand words that people use when they talk about trains. Listen as I read the book to you and see if you can hear some of these words. After I've read it, we'll take another look at the book and you can tell me the words you heard."

Josh reads the book, pointing to the words as he reads. He then takes the students back through the book and gives them time to share words they heard that relate to trains. "I heard *conductor.* That's the name of the man who was telling us to get on the train," Julie comments. Another student states, "I heard *clang.* That's the sound the bell makes." As they share words, Josh states, "You discovered several words! Let's put them on this chart so that we remember them." He creates a word display, writing "Train words" in the center. He then writes the students' words around the center, drawing a connecting line to each word.

On a second read, Josh invites students to read along. "Now that you've heard the book and taken a look at some of the words, I'll bet you can join me. I'll start the reading and you join in when you want." He then proceeds to take students through the book a second time.

To close the lesson, Josh states, "You are excellent readers! You read the text; you found some words that tell about trains. And you did something else good readers do: You read the book more than once! We're going to use this book for the next few days but I'll leave it here in the reading center just in case you want to read it on your own during independent reading time."

Terrific Texts for *Shared Reading*

Title	Author (Last, First)	Publisher/Year	ISBN
Captain Flinn and the Pirate Dinosaurs: Missing Treasure!	Andreae, Giles	Margaret K. McElderry Books/2007	9781416967453
The Little Yellow Leaf	Berger, Carin	Greenwillow/2008	9780061452246
Gingerbread Friends	Brett, Jan	G.P. Putnam's Sons/2008	9780399251610
Bedtime at the Swamp	Crow, Kristyn	HarperCollins/2008	9780060839512
The Wolves Are Back	George, Jean	Dutton/2008	9781430105909
My Dog Lyle	Goldfinger, Jennifer	Clarion/2007	9780618639830
Off Go Their Engines. Off Go Their Lights	Milusich, Janice	Dutton/2008	9780525479406
Here, Kitty, Kitty! / Ven, Gatita, Ven!	Mora, Pat	Rayo/2008	9780060850449
Goodnight Goon: A Petrifying Parody	Rex, Michael	G.P. Putnam's Sons/2008	9780399245343
Hey Mr. Choo-choo, Where Are You Going?	Wickberg, Susan	G.P. Putnam's Sons/2008	9780399239939

Winning Websites

www.ngsp.com/Products/ESLELD/nbspnbspBigBooksforESLELD /tabid/82/Default.aspx provides sets of big books for specific grade levels that have been selected with ELLs in mind.

www.teacherbigbooks.com promises to save teachers a tremendous amount of time by giving a compilation of all big books available for purchase online. Search the site by title, author, or catalog format.

Handy Hints

1. Once students are familiar with the enlarged text, provide them with smaller versions of the same text and provide time for them to practice reading the book either alone or with interested others. Students might want to assign different parts to one another.

2. Encourage children to innovate on the text by giving them a sentence frame used in the text and having them fill in their own words to finish it. One fourth-grade teacher we know used Bill Martin's *Brown Bear, Brown Bear What Do You See?* (1970) as a way to launch students writing about different states.

Fill the Gaps

Instructional Information

Predicting and understanding the use of context clues enhances *emerging* ELLs' comprehension and vocabulary development and *Fill the Gaps* is an oral reading strategy designed to do just that. By providing scaffolding and support to "fill the gaps" during a cloze reading activity, teachers can assist students' use of context clues for comprehension, vocabulary development (Hadaway, Vardell, and Young 2002), and experimentation with onset and rime (Cunningham, Hall, and Sigmon 1999). Cloze reading can be used with big books, picture books, and text selections written on sentence strips or overhead transparencies as pre-, during, and postreading activities to highlight specific vocabulary, predicting, and using context clues. These activities help students to contextualize vocabulary as they see the teacher modeling how to predict the missing word or portion of word. Additionally, allowing students to join in predicting and using vocabulary from their first language to support their listening comprehension, everyday (BICS) and academic (CALP) language provides them with a nonthreatening opportunity to begin utilizing their first language literacy skills as a tool for their English acquisition.

Savvy Suggestions

1. Select a book that has vocabulary and/or onset and rime combinations you wish to emphasize.

2. Using this book, select five to seven words to be used for the cloze activity. Write each word on a card with an accompanying illustration. Place a sticky note over each word when it appears in the text, leaving the first letter exposed.

3. Make the word cards visible to all students by placing them on the word wall or board.

4. Introduce each word by pointing to and pronouncing it.

5. Model taking a picture walk through the text. Show and explain to students that some words are covered with a sticky and that you are going to model using your background knowledge, context clues, and the displayed vocabulary cards to predict the unknown words.

6. Read the text and model selecting a word that does not make sense in the cloze. Point to the cloze vocabulary card with the illustration and ask students to tell a partner why it wouldn't work. Solicit volunteers to share their ideas.

7. Read the same passage again and model your thinking aloud as you use context clues to select the correct word. Point to the word card and move it next to the sticky and show students how to cross-check.

8. Read the next cloze passage and hold up two vocabulary cards (one of them being the correct card). Ask students to talk with a partner about what card they think fills the gap before volunteering to share their thinking with the class.

9. Read the succeeding cloze passages as described previously.

10. Place cloze activity and vocabulary cards at the reading center for students to read in small groups, partners, or individually.

Classroom Conversations

Elizabeth is starting a money unit in math and has set up a grocery store center in which students can role play buying and selling groceries. This unit causes her to select a text that she can use to highlight grocery vocabulary during whole-group reading time using *Fill the Gaps*. Elizabeth has eighteen ELLs in her second-grade classroom, most of whom learned Spanish as their first language. Recognizing that native language literacy knowledge and skills can transfer and be used to support acquisition of their second language, English, she selects a book that includes rhyming, context clues, and both English and Spanish for her *emerging* ELLs. Elizabeth selects seven words in *Bebe Goes Shopping* (Elya 2006) and creates cards with illustrations for the cloze reading. She tapes these cards to the board and introduces them to the students once they have settled themselves in the whole-group reading area.

She starts by pointing to the illustration and word *store* on the first vocabulary card and continues this process with the remaining words. Elizabeth then takes a brisk picture walk through the book, pointing out that some of the words are partially covered by a sticky note and telling the students that they are going to use their background knowledge, context clues, and vocabulary cards to predict the covered words. "Let me show you what I mean," she tells them. She reads the first sentence, "A day at the market, a really big s_____—the supermercado—with groceries galore." After looking at the displayed words, she says, "Hmm, I think the word that fills the gap is . . . *rice*! Let me read it again to check. 'A day at the market, a really big rice—the supermercado—with groceries galore.' Do you think that is right? Turn and talk to a neighbor about it." Once their talking subsides, Elizabeth invites volunteers to share their ideas. Sarah says, "*Rice* doesn't start with *s*, and *s* is the first letter of the word that is covered by the sticky." Elizabeth agrees saying, "You're right. I guess I need to look for a word that starts with an *s*. I also know that this is a rhyming book, and *rice* doesn't rhyme with *galore*. Hmm, I think it might be *store*." She repeats the passage with the word *store*, asks the students if they agree, and then pulls the sticky off the page to cross-check commenting, "This word sounds right but I think I'll put it right under the word to see if it has the same letters." Cross-checking completed, she comments, "Yes, this word is the correct one. It sounds right, looks right, and it makes sense."

Elizabeth proceeds to the next passage reading, "'Bebe in the shopping cart, high in the seat, looks all around for a dulce—a s_____.'" Elizabeth holds up the *sweet* card and the *jar* card and asks, "Should we fill the gap with *sweet* or *jar*? Tell your partner what you think." After talking with his partner, Julio volunteers, "*Dulce* is *sweet* in Spanish." Elizabeth encourages Julio to cross-check using the same procedure she used to cross-check the previous word. Elizabeth points out that this book has Spanish and English, so just like Julio, students can use their background knowledge to help them predict the word.

She continues with the cloze reading, allowing students to talk with partners and volunteer to point out and say the vocabulary word on the board that *fills the gap* until the book is finished.

She closes the lesson saying, "Using what we know about words, the printed letters, and asking ourselves what word would make the most sense with the rest of the words on the page is one way to figure out some words we might not recognize. You can give yourself some practice by using these cards and this book during independent reading time." She then places the book and the vocabulary cards at the reading center for students to use in small groups, with a partner, or independently.

Terrific Texts for *Fill the Gaps*

Title	Author (Last, First)	Publisher/Year	ISBN
Not So Tall for Six	Aston, Dianna	Charlesbridge/2008	9781570917059
Up, Down, and Around	Ayres, Katherine	Candlewick/2007	9780763623784
Hickory Dickory Dock	Baker, Keith	Harcourt/2007	9780152058180
Bebe Goes Shopping	Elya, Susan	Harcourt/2006	9780152061425
F Is for Fiesta	Elya, Susan	G.P. Putnam's Sons/2006	9780399242250
Twenty-Six Princesses	Horowitz, Dave	G.P. Putnam's Sons/2008	9780399246074
This Is the Feast	Shore, Diane	HarperCollins/2008	9780066237947
I Love Cats	Stainton, Sue	Katherine Tegen/2007	9780060851545
Come Rhyme with Me!	Wilhelm, Hans	Scholastic/2008	9780545045377
Truck Stuck	Wolf, Sallie	Charlesbridge/2008	9781580891196

Winning Websites

http://bogglesworldesl.com/cloze_activities.htm provides cloze activities grouped in three general categories: holiday, children, and adult.

www.learnnc.org/reference/2073 gives several ways to use cloze activities in the classroom.

www.associatedcontent.com/article/674995/cloze_activities_a_helpful_addition.html provides examples of a cloze activity in a teacher-submitted article.

Handy Hints

1. Cloze reading activities can be used in many different lessons to emphasize vocabulary and usage such as an emphasis on articles, prepositional phrases, position words, degrees of obligation, comparison words, or content words.

2. Cloze activities can be oral or written and cooperative or independent. Students may create their own cloze reading with a partner by covering self-selected vocabulary with sticky notes and creating vocabulary cards.

3. Providing word banks or vocabulary cards for students to use for filling the gaps is common practice as is leaving the first letter of selected words exposed. As students become more adept with this activity, the entire word can be covered and word cards can be removed.

Draw, Tell, and Listen

Instructional Information

Perhaps one of the best ways for children to learn language is to use it in authentic contexts (Snow, Burns, and Griffin 1998). *Draw, Tell, and Listen* enables them to do just that. As a result of listening to the teacher read a text segment, students draw a key idea, tell their neighbor what it is and why they drew it, and listen to their neighbor share the same. While the activity uses oral reading to convey to students how authors use language, it also capitalizes on the other language arts. Students listen for a specific purpose and use visual representation and speaking to complete the activity. The combination of these language arts ensures that all students, including *emerging level ELLs,* further develop their ability to converse with one another (i.e., BICS) as well as develop academic vocabulary (i.e., CALP) by hearing how it is used in the text. In fact, Lesaux and Geva (2006) offer a synthesis of research findings that point to the importance of oral language proficiency on ELLs' reading comprehension and cite listening comprehension as one necessary component.

Savvy Suggestions

1. Select a text that has logical stopping points that will enable students to draw, tell, and write something about the given text segment.

2. Create a simple listening guide that students can use to record their drawings.

3. Introduce the text to the students and explain how to use the listening guide.

4. Explain to students that the purpose for this activity is to help them better understand what they have heard and to help them develop a larger listening vocabulary.

5. Begin reading the book and stop after given segments.

6. Instruct students to draw something they recall from the segment you just read, turn to a neighbor and share their drawings by stating why they drew what they drew, and listen to a neighbor share theirs. Model the procedure using the first text segment.

7. Continue reading until all sections of the listening guide are completed.

8. Place the book in the reading center for students to read independently.

Classroom Conversations

As part of a larger unit on explorers, Paul selected *John Muir: America's First Environmentalist* (Lasky 2006). Recognizing that he has some *emerging language learners* in his classroom, Paul recognizes that he will need to provide students with much support so that they can comprehend the text. He decides to use *Draw, Tell, and Listen* because students will be able to use several different modalities to develop and show their understanding. After engaging students in a discussion of explorers, Paul introduces the book *John Muir* stating, "One of the explorers you are going to be learning about is John Muir. The author of this text gives you a lot of information. You might not be able to remember all of it but I have an idea that will help you to remember some of it!" Paul then instructs his students to create a listening guide by folding a paper into four parts and labeling each part with four of the major headings: Scotland, 1838; America, 1849; The War Years, 1861–1866; Journey to Florida, 1867. "Now that you have your listening guide ready, here's what you do." Paul then explains that he will read a segment and students are to draw one detail about it and be ready to share it with a neighbor. He proceeds reading aloud the first segment and models for the students what they should do saying, "I'm going to draw a *scoocher*. Remember what that is? It's a dangerous stunt or a dare. One of them that John and his brother did was to hang from their bedroom windowsill." After students have had time to draw, tell, and listen, he asks for volunteers to share their ideas. Sylvia begins by showing her drawing and stating, "I drew these ruined castles because these were part of Scotland." Pablo shares, "I drew a picture of money because it said that John liked money." "You have the idea," Paul comments. He then continues reading the remaining sections of the text in like manner. He closes the lesson stating, "We can sometimes use drawing, talking, and listening to better understand. Understanding is what listening and reading are all about. We'll continue reading about John Muir tomorrow and use *Draw, Tell, and Listen* for the next four sections in the book."

Terrific Texts for *Draw, Tell, and Listen*

Title	Author (Last, First)	Publisher/Year	ISBN
Woof! Woof!	Carter, David	Little Simon/2006	9781416908050
Holly's Red Boots	Chessa, Francesca	Holiday House/2008	9780823421589
Surprising Sharks	Davies, Nicola	Candlewick/2003	9780763621858
Old Bear	Henkes, Kevin	Greenwillow/2008	9780061552069
That Book Woman	Henson, Heather	Atheneum/2008	9781416908128
John Muir: America's First Environmentalist	Lasky, Kathryn	Candlewick/2006	9780763619572
Bats at the Library	Lies, Brian	Houghton Mifflin/2008	9780618999231
Emma Kate	Polacco, Patricia	Puffin Books/2005	9780142411964
I'm the Best Artist in the Ocean	Sherry, Kevin	Dial/2008	9780803732551
The 3 Bears and Goldilocks	Willey, Margaret	Atheneum/2008	9781416924944

Winning Websites

http://tesl-ej.org/ej17/m3.html lists several websites designed to assist ELLs. Along with a brief annotation is a sample activity from the featured website.

www.podcastsinenglish.com/index.htm enables students to use podcasts to learn English. Simply click on the level you want and choose the podcast you want students to hear.

www.manythings.org is filled with fun activities for ELLs and native English speakers, too. Word games, word puzzles, proverbs, and computer-assisted language learning activities are sure to enhance students' abilities to understand and use English for a variety of purposes.

Handy Hints

1. One way to modify *Draw, Tell, and Listen* is to use an easier text such as *Holly's Red Boots* (Chessa 2008). Students can fold their paper into four parts and draw the different red objects that appear throughout the book.

2. Students can create a riddle that describes an object and read it to either a partner or a small group. Participants can draw what they think the riddle describes, share their idea with others, and listen as others share their ideas. The reader can then reveal the object that coincides with the riddle.

Think-Aloud, Think Along, Think Alone

Instructional Information

Using the *Think-Aloud, Think Along, Think Alone* is one way to help students better understand what readers do when they read. It is a scaffolded way to use a think-aloud. The teacher first verbalizes his thoughts while reading aloud as students first listen and watch (*think-aloud*). They then participate with the teacher (*think along*) and finally think on their own (*think alone*). Given that students at the *emerging level* can understand phrases and short sentences, and given that these students are continually developing their academic vocabularies, this strategy supports them as they attempt to acquire additional skills that will enhance their comprehension. Davey (1983) identified five strategies that often need to be explicitly taught: predicting, forming mental images while reading, using prior knowledge, self-monitoring, and attending to problems when comprehension breaks down. Each strategy can be taught using the *Think-Aloud, Think Along, Think Alone* oral reading strategy.

The findings of several researchers investigating the think-aloud strategy reveal that it is an effective way to help students comprehend (Davey 1983; Bauman, Jones, and Seifert-Kessell 1993). The findings pertaining to ELLs are just as convincing. The think-aloud strategy is a useful way to better understand, teach, and engage readers (Fitzgerald 1993; Lavadenz 2003). McKeown and Gentilucci (2007) note that the think-aloud strategy is advantageous for ELLs because it enables them to stop and explore a text they are reading.

Savvy Suggestions

1. Think about the particular strategy you want to demonstrate to your students using a think-aloud. If you want to show how to self-monitor, for example, select a text to read aloud that contains

some points that will pose difficulties (e.g., unknown words, ambiguous text). Preread the text so that you have an idea of where you will stop and do your think-aloud.

2. Enlarge the text for all to see using overhead transparencies or an Elmo projector. You could also provide students with individual copies.

3. Introduce the text to the students and then begin reading aloud while students follow along.

4. Continue reading until you come to your first trouble spot and think through it aloud while students listen to what you say.

5. Resume reading until you come to another trouble spot you have identified. This time, ask students to think along with you. You might prompt them by saying something such as, "What question would you ask yourself to figure out what this part means?"

6. Continue reading giving students additional practice with thinking along.

7. Once you feel that they have an understanding of how to think aloud, invite them to think alone as they continue reading on their own.

Classroom Conversations

Valerie selects *Roberto Walks Home* (Keats and Harrington 2008) to demonstrate the *Think-Aloud, Think Along, Think Alone* strategy to her second graders. Her ultimate goal is to help all children, including the six ELL students who appear to be functioning at the *emerging level*, understand that readers are always thinking when reading and that is what enables comprehension to occur. She decides to use *Roberto Walks Home* because several of her students will be able to relate to the story. Many have older siblings and many walk or ride the bus to and from school. She begins by looking at the cover and reads it aloud. She then asks, "How many of you are like Roberto? How many of you walk home?" After students share their ideas, she states, "Just by looking at this cover, I know that Roberto is going to be walking home. What I don't know is why he'll be walking home. Is this how he usually gets home? Well, I guess I'll just have to read to get my question answered." She then opens the book and begins reading. After reading the first two pages, she stops and says, "Hmmmm. I still don't know the answer to my question but I have another one. It says the Roberto is waiting while the other kids go home. Who is he waiting for? Well, maybe if I keep reading I'll find out." She turns the page and reads it aloud saying, "Oh, I see! He usually walks home with Peter but today he's not going to because he's waiting for his brother, Miguel. The text tells me right here." She reads the next few pages and then stops saying, "I'm getting the idea that Roberto is getting tired of waiting for his brother. Think with me. What is giving me this idea?" Steven comments, "Well, he's looking a little sad." Valerie responds, "Yes, sometimes readers use pictures just like you did to understand what's going on." Angela adds, "The words also say that he was looking up and down the street. I did this when I had to wait for my *Abuela* to pick me up from school yesterday." Taking Angela's lead, Valerie comments, "So you used the words to help you understand what is happening." Valerie continues the reading, stopping along the way to invite students to think along with her so that they can better understand the text.

She concludes the lesson by stating, "Readers are always thinking when they are reading. Thinking is important because it helps the reader to understand the text. Without understanding, there really is no reading. Now that you have had some practice thinking with me, I'm going to give you some practice thinking alone when you read with me in small-group reading today."

Terrific Titles for *Think-Aloud, Think Along, Think Alone*

Title	Author (Last, First)	Publisher/Year	ISBN
To Be a Kid	Ajmera, Maya Ivanko, John	Charlesbridge/1999	9780881068412
Turkey Bowl	Bildner, Phil	Simon & Schuster/2008	9780689878961

Title	Author (Last, First)	Publisher/Year	ISBN
Market Day	Cordsen, Carol	Dutton/2008	9780525478836
Alfred Digs	George, Lindsay	Greenwillow/2008	9780060787608
Oh, Brother!	Grimes, Nikki	Greenwillow/2006	9780688172954
The Way Back Home	Jeffers, Oliver	Philomel/2007	9780399250743
Roberto Walks Home	Keats, Ezra Jack Harrington, Janice	Viking/2008	9780670063161
Hen Hears Gossip	McDonald, Megan	Greenwillow/2008	9780061138775
Splat the Cat	Scotton, Rob	HarperCollins/2008	9780007284542
The 3 Bears and Goldilocks	Willey, Margaret	Atheneum/2008	9781416924944

Winning Websites

www.readwritethink.org has a lesson entitled "Building Comprehension Through Think-Alouds." It offers some additional ideas for designing and using think-alouds.

http://wvde.state.wv.us/strategybank/ThinkAloud.html is filled with additional information about think-alouds. Among this information is a video clip of a reading specialist modeling a think-aloud.

www.literacymatters.org/content/study/think.htm includes information about think-alouds. This site provides additional websites and resources that describe think-aloud strategies.

Handy Hints

1. To help students remember specific fix-up strategies before and during reading, Block and Israel (2004) suggest providing students with bookmarks that contain some reminders. Reminders include revising original predictions, asking questions, and

determining word meanings. Students can use the bookmarks throughout the reading of a given text.

2. Using a reverse think-aloud (Block 1997) is another way to change up this activity. Instead of being told what the teacher is thinking, students ask. As with the original think-aloud, the teacher begins by asking students to read along silently while he reads aloud. However, they can stop the teacher at any time and ask, "So what are you thinking?" The teacher then responds.

Chime Right In

Instructional Information

Choral reading is an inclusive and low-anxiety activity that all students can do without fearing failure or tension. In addition to being enjoyable for all learners, a great deal of research has been conducted on its effectiveness. The benefits of choral reading include improved self-confidence (Harste, Short, and Burke 1988), greater enjoyment and interest in reading (Miccinati 1985; Woodbury 1979), increased fluency including rate and prosody from multiple readings of a text (Bradley and Thalgott 1987; Chomsky 1976; Schreiber 1980), and vocabulary development (Sampson, Allen, and Sampson 1991; Templeton 1991). In addition to all of the previously mentioned benefits, there are four factors present in choral reading that are specific to enhancing second language acquisition: low-anxiety learning environments (Gardner and Lambert 1972; Krashen 1983; Ovando and Collier 1985), repeated practice (Krashen 1982; Schreiber 1980), comprehensible input (Krashen 1983; Krashen and Terrell 1983), and drama (Hernandez 1989; Nomura 1985). These findings, along with the enjoyment found in choral reading, provide plenty of evidence for using choral reading with *emerging* ELLs.

Chime Right In is the ultimate scaffolding for ELLs because it provides low-anxiety, repeated practice with texts while incorporating comprehensible input and drama. The texts are carefully selected and adapted as necessary for ELLs functioning at the various language proficiency levels. Selecting poems or texts that deal with familiar topics or content, use rhyme, and have rhythm or humor (McCauley and McCauley 1992; Peregoy and Boyle 2008) is ideal. The text is read to students multiple times before asking students to practice and eventually perform. Adding gestures and actions can help to make the story or poem more meaningful while also enhancing the performance.

Savvy Suggestions *(adapted from McCauley and McCauley 1992; Peregoy
and Boyle 2008)*

1. Select an appropriate text that may be slightly beyond what students can read independently. Patterned, rhyming, rhythmic, humorous, and texts with familiar content that lend themselves to gestures or actions are ideal.

2. Create actions or gestures to reinforce the meaning of the story.

3. Read the text to the students multiple times using enlarged text for all to see or providing students with copies so they can follow along. While reading, demonstrate the actions or gestures that accompany the text.

4. Invite students to join you as you reread the text while pointing to the words on the chart or overhead transparency.

5. Repeat step 4, but add gestures and actions and invite students to join in.

6. Continue practicing with greater emphasis on prosody and actions until all students feel comfortable and participate.

Classroom Conversations

Benjamin is a fifth-grade teacher who is beginning a unit on American history. For the unit introduction, he has decided to use *America: My Land, Your Land, Our Land* (Nikola-Lisa 1997) during a *Chime Right In* activity for three reasons. First, he wants to provide a meaningful and low-anxiety experience for his *emerging* ELLs in fifth grade to access the content and vocabulary. Second, he wants to use the artwork and rhythmic text as a catalyst to begin an introductory discussion about the joys and beauty of America as well as the underlying tensions. Third, he wants to use the text as a theme to tie the history together as a final performance.

In order to make this experience the most meaningful for his fifth-grade students, Benjamin decides that he will create actions for a few sections of the text, but will allow students to provide input for the remaining portions at the end of the unit. Not wanting to lose the contextualization that the beautiful artwork provides, he makes overhead transparencies of the text and projects them as he reads the text aloud in addition to giving each student their own copy of the text. Benjamin begins the lesson by reading, "hot land," and fanning himself with his hand. He then proceeds to the next phrase and reads, "cold land," while making a shivering motion. Once he completes the text, he reads it again emphasizing the rhythmic text with his expression and actions. Benjamin explains to students that they will be using this text as an introduction and final performance for their American History unit and invites the students to join him in chorally reading the text shown on the overhead transparencies and to use the actions as they feel comfortable. He then asks students, "What picture and words made you think of the joys and beauty of America?" After students have a chance to talk with each other, he calls Saul, who volunteers, "rich land." The students are asked to try to create an action that represents this concept. Benjamin closes the lesson by telling students that they will be creating actions and practicing throughout the unit as they make connections between their *Chime Right In* performance and what they learn in their textbook. He comments, "Reading is all about understanding what you read. One way to show your understanding is to create actions like we just did and you will do throughout this unit."

Terrific Texts for *Chime Right In*

Title	Author (Last, First)	Publisher/Year	ISBN
Doggone Dogs	Beaumont, Karen	Dial/2008	9780803731578
Jack's House	Beil, Karen	Holiday House/2008	9780823419135
The Pout-Pout Fish	Diesen, Deborah	Farrar, Straus & Giroux/2008	9780374360962
Mother Goose Numbers on the Loose	Dillon, Leo Dillon, Diane	Harcourt/2007	9780152056766

Title	Author (Last, First)	Publisher/Year	ISBN
Where's My Mom?	Donaldson, Julia	Dial/2008	9780803732285
Jack and Jill's Treehouse	Edwards, Pamela	Katherine Tegen Books/ 2008	9780060090777
Beetle Bop	Fleming, Denise	Harcourt/2007	9780152059361
All Aboard for Dreamland!	Harby, Melanie	Simon & Schuster/2007	9781896580487
In the Night Garden	Joosse, Barbara	Henry Holt & Company/ 2008	9780805066715
America: My Land, Your Land, Our Land	Nikola-Lisa, W.	Lee & Low Books/1997	9781880000373

Winning Websites

www.readwritethink.org/lessons/lesson_view.asp?id=69 provides lesson plans incorporating poetry and choral reading.

http://teachersmentor.com/readingk3/using_poetry.html provides links to poetry sites, ideas on how to use poetry and choral reading, suggestions for how to choose poems, and management tips.

www.readingrockets.org/article/3416 has an article that provides guidelines for instruction, suggestions for text and other activities.

Handy Hints

Humorous poetry and many repetitive texts can be used for choral reading. The teacher can create actions and gestures to use with these texts. Older or more advanced students can create their own actions and even select their own texts. Performances might range from in-class practice to performing for other students, classes, or parents, once all students feel confident.

Using Oral Reading with Developing Language Learners (Level 3)

The second graders put their coats and lunches in their lockers and stroll into our classroom, all the while talking with one another. Just like other days, today starts with a ten-minute talking period during which the students talk with one another and with me (Michael). This time of the day is special to me because I get to know things about students I probably wouldn't otherwise. I also firmly believe that students learn language by using it in a variety of ways. Today the students are talking with one another as I walk around and listen in. I overhear Josh talking to Danelle, a developing ELL, about their mothers. The conversation goes something like this: Josh says to Danelle, "My mom is a Sagittarius." Danelle pauses, looks at Josh as if to question what he means but instead offers, "Really? My mom is a vegetarian." Josh, looking a little surprised by Danelle's comment, accepts it nonetheless by commenting, "Oh." Hardly able to contain my laughter, I leave, chuckling my way to another group. How, I wonder, might I be able to clarify the meaning of both terms for both children?

As this brief scenario illustrates, *developing ELLs* are showing signs of knowing much about English. Feeling more at ease and participating in different school activities have helped them to understand and use more complex speech than they did in the previous two levels. They even begin to use English spontaneously but, as in the example at the beginning of this chapter, they may not have a full understanding of the words they choose to use. Likewise, they might find it difficult to express themselves because they are still acquiring vocabulary and an understanding of how to phrase sentences. Nonetheless, they are able to converse with others using sentences that are comprehensible yet sometimes awkwardly worded.

Make no mistake, however. *Developing ELLs* are on their way to becoming proficient readers yet, like all children, they vary in their reading ability. One way to support their growth is to use texts that enable them to use their background knowledge when reading. Another way is to use purposeful oral reading strategies designed to help them develop specific skills in nonthreatening ways. Figure 5–1 is an overview of appropriate oral reading strategies this chapter show-cases. Teachers can use these strategies when designing instruction to help *developing ELLs* better comprehend English.

	Strategies				
Reading Skills	Find the Signs	How Do I Feel?	Read with Me	What's the Word?	Listen to Me
Positive Attitudes/Interest in Reading	•	•	•	•	•
Reading Comprehension	•	•	•		
Listening Comprehension				•	•
Social Vocabulary		•	•	•	•
Academic Vocabulary			•	•	•
Use of Language Cues	•	•	•	•	•
Predicting				•	
Forming Images					
Using Prior Knowledge		•		•	
Monitoring			•		•
Inferring	•	•		•	
Fluency (R = rate, A = accuracy, P = prosody)	P	P	R A P		R A P
Skimming					

Figure 5–1. Effective Oral Reading Strategies and Skills for Developing Language Learners

Find the Signs

Instructional Information

Typographical cues are similar to road signs. The reader, like a driver, must be able to read the signs to navigate their way through the roads or pages of text. *Find the Signs* helps *developing ELLs* do just that by emphasizing the impact that various typographical signs have on meaning. It is important to remember that like road signs, typographical signs do not look the same in every language. For example, Spanish uses speech dashes to indicate speaking instead of quotation marks (Cappellini 2005). Therefore, drawing attention to and modeling how to read typographical signs like punctuation marks, font size, bold print, underlining, italics, and various combinations of these signs helps *developing ELLs* understand the author's intended meaning. Using these cues to assist prosody development and reading comprehension are just a few of the benefits of this oral reading strategy.

Savvy Suggestions *(adapted from Opitz and Rasinski 2008)*

1. Select one or two specific typographical signs or cues that you want to introduce or highlight. Figure 5–2 lists several signs, what they mean, and examples of how they are used.

2. Write sentences from a book that has previously been read or will be read that includes the specific signs that you are going to emphasize on an overhead transparency, sentence strips, or chart paper.

3. Tell students that you want them to listen to you as read the same sentence two times because they will need to decide which reading gives them the best understanding of what is happening.

4. Read the sentence the first time using monotone voice and don't adhere to any typographical signs.

Typographical Signs	What Do They Mean?	Examples
Comma	Pause reading; placement of comma can affect meaning	Henry, my dog is happy to see you. Henry, my dog, is happy to see you.
Period	Longer pause because it marks the end of a sentence	The boy loved his new book.
Question mark	Raise intonation at the end of the question	What is that?
Exclamation mark	Read with emotion	I can't believe it!
Quotation marks	Someone is speaking	Ben said, "What are you doing?"
Underlined, enlarged, and/or bold print	Read with special stress	That is what <u>she</u> thinks. <u>That</u> is what she thinks.
Combination	Read meaningful unit with special stress	My father yelled, "**Lindsey, you get back here right now!**"

Figure 5–2. Typographical Signs and What They Mean (adapted from Opitz and Rasinski 2008)

5. Read the sentence the second time using all typographical signs.

6. Ask students which reading provided a better understanding and why. Ask students how the first reading was different from the second reading. Point out, if it wasn't already mentioned, the typographical signs in the sentence and how you used them to help you provide the audience with a better understanding of the sentence.

7. Invite students to read with a partner and try to *find the signs* in a self-selected text.

8. Have partners read aloud one sentence in which they found a sign, and have them tell what the sign indicated they needed to do when reading aloud.

Classroom Conversations

Karen notices that some of her fourth-grade students are reading in a monotone voice and ignoring typographical cues. She wants to help her *developing ELLs* understand how authors use these typographical cues as signs to help the reader understand the meaning of the text. *For You Are a Kenyan Child* (Cunnane 2006) seems like a perfect choice because it has quotation marks, question marks, bold and italicized text in varying sizes, in addition to the typical commas and periods that her students encounter on a daily basis.

She opens the lesson by reading aloud using a loud voice for the large, bold print text and changing her voice to sound like different characters when reading words in quotation marks. After reading the book, she puts up an overhead transparency of the text and says, "I am going to read this two times, and I want you to be thinking about which reading gives you the best idea of what is happening in the story." She first reads in a monotone voice without adhering to the typographical cues. The second reading includes different voices for the text found in quotations, rising intonation for the question mark, emotion for the exclamation mark, and special stress for the bold and enlarged text. Then she asks students, "Which reading provided a better understanding and why?" Saraya answers, "The second one was more exciting because you read it with voices." Juan chimes in, "Yeah, the voices were cool, but I liked it when you shouted really loud when you called out their names." Karen agrees and discusses how these typographical signs helped her understand how the author intended to convey meaning. She introduces and places a chart like Figure 5–2 on the wall for students to reference when needed.

Karen invites students to select a text with a partner. She asks students to find the signs in the text that help convey the author's intended meaning while they read aloud with their partner. Students are invited to share one sentence in which they find a sign and tell the class what the sign indicates they needed to do while reading. Karen closes the lesson by saying, "Now that you know that authors use signs to help you understand the story, you can use these clues while reading in small groups, partners, or individually."

Terrific Texts for *Find the Signs*

Title	Author (Last, First)	Publisher/Year	ISBN
The Queen of Style	Buehner, Caralyn Buehner, Mark	Dial/2008	9780803728783
Hurry! Hurry!	Bunting, Eve	Harcourt/2007	9780152054106
For You Are a Kenyan Child	Cunnane, Kelly	Atheneum/2006	9780689861949
Rainy Day!	Lakin, Patricia	Dial/2007	9780803730922
The Cardboard Piano	Perkins, Lynne	Greenwillow/2008	9780061542657
Cat & Mouse	Schoenherr, Ian	Greenwillow/2008	9780061363139
Gobble Gobble Crash! A Barnyard Counting Bash	Stiegemeyer, Julie	Dutton/2008	9780525479598
Roadwork	Sutton, Sally	Candlewick/2008	9780763639129
Frederick Finch, Loudmouth	Weaver, Tess	Clarion/2008	9780618452392
Booming Bella	Williams, Carol	G.P. Putnam's Sons/2008	9780399242779

Winning Websites

http://teachers.net/lessonplans/posts/3595.html has lesson plans about the Amazon that include a *Find the Signs* activity.

www.songsforteaching.com/grammarpunctuationspelling /punctuation/periodquestionmarkcommacolonastrophe exclamation.htm links to a song that helps teach punctuation marks.

www.readwritethink.org/lessons/lesson_view.asp?id=260 provides a lesson plan using Martin Luther King Jr.'s "Letter from Birmingham Jail" to demonstrate how much meaning is carried through punctuation marks.

Handy Hints

1. Instead of presenting the students with a chart like Figure 5–2, have students create their own class chart of typographical signs that they know and find in their own reading.

2. Copy the classroom chart like Figure 5–2, but omit the examples. Have students do a *find the signs* search during their next reading, using the chart like a cloze activity. With a partner, they can try to find examples in their self-selected text of as many signs as possible.

3. Provide students with a passage that is missing all typographical signs. Ask them to work in small groups to add signs to make the passage more meaningful. Have groups share their completed passage with the class to compare how the passage could be interpreted differently when typographical signs are not present.

How Do I Feel?

Instructional Information

Proficient readers ask questions before, during, and after reading for many different reasons. Sometimes they pose questions to clarify the author's intended meaning and at other times to predict what will happen at various points in the story. At still other times, readers' questions center on the story character. Asking questions of a story character can help students better understand the character and ultimately the whole story. Paying attention to how a character feels about the changes that are occurring in the story, for example, helps readers to know and perhaps even relate to the character.

The reported findings of several researchers have indicated that while asking questions is one of several essential reading strategies that proficient readers use automatically, other children including ELLs need to be taught how (Guthrie and Taboado 2004; Duke and Pearson 2002; Shanahan and Beck 2006). *How Do I Feel?* is one strategy you can use to help children learn how to ask questions of story characters' moods and actions in an effort to boost reading comprehension.

Savvy Suggestions

1. Select a text that has one main character with which students can relate.

2. Introduce the asking questions strategy saying something such as, "When we read, we can ask questions to understand why a character is acting the way he is acting. Understanding the character's actions can help us to better understand the story and to stay interested in it."

3. Tell the students that you will be reading them a story and to pay attention to how the character is feeling and what causes the character to feel that way.

4. Stop at various points in the story to model posing questions of the character.

5. Remind students that sometimes authors have the character act in certain ways to show how the character is feeling. Instead of saying that the character is mad, for example, the author might have the character yell or throw something.

Classroom Conversations

Interacting with her third graders during a variety of reading experiences has helped Maria see what students know and need to know. Asking questions to understand characters' emotions and motives is one such strategy. After reviewing several titles with her *developing ELLs* at the forefront of her mind, she chooses *Nobody Here But Me* (Viorst 2008). She gathers the children in the whole-group meeting area and uses the five-step procedure (listed above) to carry out the lesson. She begins by stating, "Because I have been watching you read, I know that all of you are good readers. Many of you make predictions before and during reading. Others of you summarize what you have read to help you remember important ideas. I've even seen some of you stop and reread when you know that you need to in order to understand what you are reading. Today I want to show you one more strategy that readers use and it's all about asking questions." She continues, "When we read, we can ask questions to understand why a character is acting the way he is acting. Understanding the character's actions can help us to better understand the story and to stay interested in it. Let's give it a try."

She introduces *Nobody Here But Me* by showing the cover and reading the title and asking questions such as, "So who do you think *me* is? How do you think he feels? What lets you know he feels that way?" Maria continues in like manner throughout the next few pages of the story, pausing at the end of nearly every two-page spread to ask questions about the main character. After reading the next two-page spread, she asks for volunteers to share questions they might have. Roberto asks and states, "Why is he wanting everyone to pay attention to him? It seems like he thinks he is the most important person in the house."

Celina adds, "I was wondering the same thing. Why does he think his sister should stop playing with her friend and pay attention to him? I think Roberto might be right. The boy thinks he is the most important. But why does he think so?" Questions such as these help Maria see that students are understanding how to use the asking question strategy to understand story characters and that is exactly what she tells them to close the lesson. Maria tells them, "Today we have been focusing on asking questions to understand the character: why the character does what he does and how he feels about what's happening in the story. Asking questions is a perfect way to help you understand the story. It also makes the story more interesting and enjoyable."

Terrific Texts for *How Do I Feel?*

Title	Author (Last, First)	Publisher/Year	ISBN
Pete & Pickles	Breathed, Berkely	Philomel/2008	9780399250828
Humpty Dumpty Climbs Again	Horowitz, Dave	G.P. Putnam's Sons/2008	9780399247736
The Robot and the Bluebird	Lucas, David	Farrar, Straus & Giroux/2007	9781842706237
Zip, Zip . . . Homework	Poydar, Nancy	Holiday House/2008	9780823420902
It's Not Fair!	Rosenthal, Amy	HarperCollins/2008	9780061152573
The House of Joyful Living	Schotter, Roni	Melanie Kroupa Books/2008	9780374334291
The Nice Book	Stein, David	G.P. Putnam's Sons/2008	9780399250507
Nobody Here But Me	Viorst, Judith	Farrar, Straus & Giroux/2008	9780374355401
Otto Runs for President	Wells, Rosemary	Scholastic/2008	9780545037228
Art from Her Heart: Folk Artist	Whitehead, Kathy Evans, Shane	G.P. Putnam's Sons/2008	9780399242199

Winning Websites

**www.learnnc.org/search?area=best%20practices&phrase=
comprehension** is a website created by LEARN NC, a program of the
University of North Carolina at Chapel Hill School of Education. It
locates and posts innovative and successful practices in K–12 education, and offers several ideas for helping teachers enhance the comprehension of ELLs.

**www.everythingesl.net/inservices/elementary_sites_ells_71638
.php** offers an extensive list of websites designed for elementary-aged
ELLs. Websites are categorized by grade levels and each website is
briefly annotated. Ideas for helping students navigate and share information they gain from the websites are also provided.

**http://curriculum.dpsk12.org/elem_lit_program/mini-lesson_
character.pdf** provides a minilesson for understanding characters.
This minilesson includes guiding questions for scaffolding and infer-
ring when initially introducing how to use character actions and dialogue to infer.

Handy Hints

1. After students have become familiar with story characters from
   different books, put the name of the character and book in which
   the character appears on a card. Place all cards in a bag. Select a
   volunteer to draw a card out of the bag, read it silently, and to do
   some action that the character performed in the story. Have others see if they can state the name of the character and story in
   which the character appears.

2. After reading a story such as *Nobody Here But Me*, engage students in the "What if?" game. Pose questions such as, "What if
   the sister had paid attention to her brother? What if the father
   had stopped checking his email and played with his son? What if
   the boy had gotten locked in the basement when he was hiding?"

Read with Me

Instructional Information

Working with partners is particularly beneficial for ELLs because the support they receive is nonthreatening thereby providing opportunities for verbal interaction (Meyers 1993; Diaz-Rico and Weed 2002). Li and Nes (2001) reported that during a paired reading intervention in which ELLs were paired with a "skilled reader," ELLs improved their pronunciation, rate, and accuracy while reading. *Read with Me* is an oral reading strategy that incorporates a form of partner reading (also referred to as paired, buddy, or mentor reading) to help develop reading comprehension, vocabulary, fluency, and a positive attitude and interest in reading.

Students at the *developing* level can understand written English and are beginning to develop their academic language, so providing practice with partner reading activities is a perfect support to help students take risks in a nonthreatening environment. Purposefully selecting partners for *developing ELLs* creates opportunities for language partners who can either provide a strong English model or bilingual support for clarification purposes in their native language. In order for the partner reading to be most successful, the teacher models the task and expected interactions and then provides support as the students begin to practice reading aloud the selected text (Herrell and Jordan 2008). Depending on the text selection, the partner reading can provide opportunities to develop both BICS and CALP while simultaneously improving students' pronunciation, rate, and accuracy during reading.

Savvy Suggestions *(adapted from Herrell and Jordan 2008; Topping 1987)*

1. Decide the purpose of the partner reading before selecting partners for students. If you want strong modeling of English for a *developing ELL*, pair that student with a strong native English speaker. If

you want to provide native language support for clarifications and discussion, pair the *developing ELL* with a bilingual partner.

2. Select an appropriate text for reading with a student partner.

3. Model alternating reading every other page with a student volunteer partner.

4. During modeling, make various miscues and provide explicit instruction on how the partner can provide support. Tell students to give the reader a few seconds to self-correct. If the student doesn't self-correct and the miscue alters the meaning, give the students some possible questions to ask like, "Is there another word that would make more sense here?" or "What would sound better here?" or "Does that look right?"

5. Ask the student volunteer to model this questioning technique when you make miscues.

6. Pair the students according to the purpose you selected in step 1.

7. Allow students to select a text and begin *Read with Me*.

8. Provide support for student paired reading and interactions as needed.

Classroom Conversations

Julie wants to help *developing ELLs* practice oral reading in non-threatening ways while also celebrating their biliteracy. She wants to select a text with English and Spanish to support comprehension in both languages. She realizes that using *Tortillas and Lullabies, Tortillas y cancioncitas* (Reiser 1998) as a model with her second graders during *Read with Me* would be a perfect book for this purpose. When planning for this activity, she decides to create student pairs that have one native English speaker and one native Spanish speaker so that the English speakers can provide strong modeling and support for the English text and the Spanish speakers can provide strong modeling and support for the Spanish text. Both partners, then, get to be experts and utilize the questioning techniques for miscues. In order for this to work for the entire class, she creates a tub of books with Spanish and English text.

Prior to the lesson, Julie asks for a student volunteer who knows Spanish to help her model *Read with Me*. Ariana volunteers, so Julie gives her the book, *Tortillas and Lullabies, Tortillas y cancioncitas* (Reiser 1998), to practice reading during independent reading and at home. After providing Ariana with time and practice to become familiar with the book, Julie and Ariana model the procedures listed previously. Julie opens the lesson by saying, "Ariana has been very brave and volunteered to be my *Read with Me* partner. We are going to show you how we read together and what to do if your partner makes a miscue." Julie starts by reading the first page and makes a pronunciation miscue when reading the word *bisabuela* (great-grandmother). She says, "If I make a miscue that doesn't change the meaning, then Ariana can just let me keep reading. If I make a miscue that does change the meaning and I don't correct it, then Ariana can ask me one of the following questions: 'Is there another word that would make more sense here?'; 'What would sound better here?' 'Does that look right?'" Julie writes these questions on the board for students to see. She then asks Ariana if she is going to ask one of the questions, but Ariana says, "No, Miss. You didn't say it quite right, but it still means the same." Ariana reads the next page with no miscues. Julie reads the third page and replaces *mama* with *bebe* and doesn't self-correct. Ariana says, "Does that look right? *Bebe* starts with a *b*." Julie makes the correction and they continue reading in this manner for the next couple of pages until Ariana has modeled using all three miscue questions.

Julie then tells the students who their partner will be for this activity. Julie places the tub of books with English and Spanish writing on the front table. She allows the partners to select a text of their choice from the tub and to start reading. After walking around the room and providing support when needed, Julie closes the lesson by saying, "Wow! You are all experts. We are going to use these books to practice being the reader and asking your partner questions all week during *Read with Me* time."

Terrific Texts for *Read with Me*

Title	Author (Last, First)	Publisher/Year	ISBN
Now & Ben: The Modern Inventions of Benjamin Franklin	Barretta, Gene	Henry Holt & Company/ 2006	9780805079173
Goodnight Moon 123/ Buenas noches, luna 123	Brown, Margaret	Rayo/2007	9780061173257
Teeth	Collard, Sneed	Charlesbridge/2008	9781580891202
Come Fly with Me	Ichikawa, Satomi	Philomel/2008	9780399246791
Grandma Calls Me Beautiful	Joosse, Barbara	Chronicle/2008	9780811858151
Peter Spit a Seed at Sue	Koller, Jackie	Viking/2008	9780670063093
Spark the Firefighter	Krensky, Stephen	Dutton/2008	9780525478874
Dogfessions: Secret Confessions from Dogs	Moustaki, Nikki	HarperCollins/2008	9780061575617
Tortillas and Lullabies, Tortillas y cancioncitas	Reiser, Lynn	Greenwillow/1998	9780688146283
Building Manhattan	Vila, Laura	Viking/2008	9780670062843

Winning Websites

www.freetranslation.com is a website that will convert books created by children into the first language of other children.

www.colorincolorado.org is a website for educators and families. It is a bilingual site with information about books and authors, research, reports, and various other topics about how to help ELLs be successful.

www.magickeys.com/books provides free online children's storybooks.

Handy Hints

1. Another way to use partner reading is to have an older student who needs to learn basic reading vocabulary partner up with a younger student. The older student needs to be able to read the text to be used when reading with the younger student who needs additional help with reading. The advantage to this type of pairing is that the older student gets additional practice in identifying words with integrity. In other words, reading a book that might otherwise be seen as too childish becomes acceptable because it appears that the reading is being done primarily for the benefit of the younger student.

2. Provide time for students to create their own books to read with a partner. Partners can alternate using different languages when writing the book. They can then read their pages to one another.

What's the Word?

Instructional Information

Children learn many words by hearing them in meaningful contexts (Elley 1989). The same is true when reading. Assuming that they know most of the words that surround an unknown word, students can use the context to decipher the meaning of an unknown word even if they cannot pronounce it correctly. However, according to Schifini (2006), ELLs may find using context difficult for a couple of reasons. First, they might not know enough words that surround the key words they want or need to know. Second, they may have limited command of the English language. The good news is that there is evidence that ELLs can be explicitly taught vocabulary and how to use context clues to determine word meanings, both of which increase their comprehension (Shanahan and Beck 2006). *What's the Word?* is designed to help students learn how to use context clues in general, and definition context clues in particular. It is a necessary and appropriate skill for ELLs functioning at the *developing level* because it expands on what they already know about the English language. Learning additional vocabulary and how to use context clues to determine the meaning of unknown words increases their ability to use academic vocabulary across all content areas. In order to meet with success when using *What's the Word?*, remember to use texts that enable students to use their background knowledge.

Savvy Suggestions

1. Select an appropriate text that will enable you to demonstrate the desired learning. Keep in mind that there are six types of context clues. Teaching one at a time makes student success more likely.

2. Prepare sentence strips that contain examples of the context clue you will be teaching.

3. Provide students with some background for the text.

4. Read the whole text.

5. Revisit the text and specific sentence strips.

6. Discuss with students how to use the author's words to figure out the meaning of new words.

7. Provide plenty of practice.

Classroom Conversations

Eduardo has noticed that his second graders are becoming proficient readers. However, his observations have led him to conclude that nearly all of the students need some help with learning how to use context clues to understand better the meanings of the key words that impact their comprehension of a text. Paying attention to the fact that he has some *developing ELLs* in his classroom, he selects *Tooth on the Loose* (Elya 2008) and designs a lesson focused on learning how to use definitional context clues (i.e., when the author defines a word that may be unknown). Recognizing that students will be more successful if they first hear the entire story, he introduces it, telling students to listen for words they already know. He then reads it aloud. Once finished, he revisits the text and focuses on showing students how to use definitional context clues.

Eduardo comments, "Now that you have heard the whole story, let's revisit it. I want to show you what the author did to help the reader understand some of the Spanish words she uses to write the text." Turning to the second page of the story, he rereads, "My brother—hermano—." He then directs students to the displayed sentence strip on which he has printed the sentence. He states, "I'm wondering if anyone knows what the word *hermano* means." Celina volunteers, "I know a lot of Spanish words. It means *brother*." Eduardo comments, "Yes, many times we can use what we know to read words. Sometimes you will be reading books that have new information and you might not be able to use too much of what you know. This is when you need to know how to use the words you *do* know to figure out those you don't. Sometimes the author helps you out by giving you the definition either before or after the word." Directing students' attention to the sentence strip again, he continues, "Take a look at this sentence. Look what the author did! She starts by saying 'My brother,' Then, she gives the Spanish word for *brother*. Right away, I can understand that *hermano* means brother! I might not be able to pronounce it the right way, but I know what the word means." Eduardo continues the lesson using other examples from the text, giving students plenty of practice. He concludes the lesson by saying, "Using words you know and hints from the author can often help you to figure out important words so that you can understand what you are reading. And remember! Understanding is what reading is all about."

Terrific Texts for *What's the Word?*

Title	Author (Last, First)	Publisher/Year	ISBN
Big Words for Little People	Curtis, Jamie Lee	HarperCollins/2008	9780061127601
Papa and Me	Dorros, Arthur	Rayo/2008	9780060581572
Oh No, Gotta Go!	Elya, Susan	G.P. Putnam's Sons/2003	9780399234934
Tooth on the Loose	Elya, Susan	G.P. Putnam's Sons/2008	9780399244599
Butterfly, Butterfly	Horacek, Petr	Candlewick/2007	9780763633431
Can You Say Peace?	Katz, Karen	Henry Holt & Company/2006	9780805078930
Flip, Float, Fly Seeds on the Move	Macken, JoAnn	Holiday House/2008	9780823420438
Fancy Nancy's Favorite Fancy Words from Accessories to Zany	O'Conner, Jane	HarperCollins/2008	9780061549236
Trouts Are Made of Trees	Sayre, April	Charlesbridge/2008	9781580891370
Tiny Tortilla	Williams, Arlene	Dutton/2005	9780525473824

Winning Websites

http://searchlight.utexas.org/content/serp-secondary/activities /types-of-context-clues/view?SearchableText=secondary& search=true&Subj=None provides more information about context clues with accompanying video clips and other interactive activities.

www.englishclub.net provides grammar and vocabulary activities and word games. It also offers free printables for ELL teachers.

www.rhymezone.com has a rhyming dictionary and a thesaurus. Locating words associated with a given word is fairly easy. Simply type in the word and this site will retrieve corresponding synonyms, antonyms, rhyming words, quotations, and pictures.

Handy Hints

Creating *What's the Word?* riddles is one way to help children learn new words and how context can be used to decipher them. Consider using this procedure, which is adapted from *Quick Activities to Build a Very Voluminous Vocabulary* (Nickerson 1998):

1. Display and read a riddle aloud and ask students to guess the answer: "I am a color. You see me on ripe bananas. I am also the color of some fall leaves. What's the word?" (Answer: yellow)

2. Have students point out any clues that gave away the answer.

3. Provide time for students to create their own riddles.

4. In turn, have students share their riddles with the whole class, a small group, or a partner. As each is solved, ask students how they figured out the answer.

Listen to Me

Instructional Information

Reading aloud can be intimidating, especially when readers have no say in what they have to read. As Krashen (1982, 1983) emphasizes, for optimal learning and language acquisition, the affective filter must be low and students must have opportunities for repeated practice. *Listen to Me* helps do just that by creating a low-anxiety environment in which *developing ELLs* have choice and repeated practice before sharing with a group of peers. *Listen to Me* encourages students to read a passage multiple times, select their favorite section, and practice it with a partner before reading to the group and explaining why they chose it. For *developing ELLs,* this is perfect because they are fairly comfortable engaging in social conversations and are beginning to develop their academic language proficiency. This oral reading activity facilitates the use and development of both BICS and CALP using a challenging text while providing scaffolding and practice to ensure that students will meet with success.

Savvy Suggestions *(adapted from Boyd-Batstone 2006; Opitz and Rasinski 2008)*

1. Select a text that students have read, and have students look back through the text for their favorite sentence or paragraph. Any type of text may be used for this activity.

2. Ask students to mark their favorite selection using a sticky or sheet of paper.

3. Ask students to practice reading their selection to a partner at least two times. Remind students that they can help each other with difficult words.

4. Tell students that you are going to call on a volunteer to share their favorite passage, but after the first volunteer they can take cues from each other to take their turn.

5. Allow students to read their favorite passages until everyone who wanted to share has had an opportunity. While one student reads, the rest simply listen rather than follow along.

6. Ask students to share why their selection was important to them.

Classroom Conversations

Ty wants to inspire critical thinking and meaningful reading of nonfiction texts while also helping to develop social and academic language in his third-grade classroom. Knowing that his *developing ELLs* still need support and opportunities to practice with feedback before independent reading for an audience, he decides to use *Elephants of Africa* (Gibbons 2008) in the *Listen to Me* activity. He introduces the lesson by saying, "We all read *Elephants of Africa* last week during small-group reading, so today I would like you to look back through your books and mark your favorite sentence or paragraph with a sticky." After the students have all placed their stickies in the book, he tells them to practice reading their favorite part to a partner at least two times and reminds them that partners can help each other with difficult words. He gives them time to practice and then says, "After I call on the first volunteer, you can take cues from each other and read your favorite passage when no one else is reading. Remember that when you are not reading, you are listening to the reader. Who would like to volunteer?" Lupe raises her hand and reads, "Tusks start to grow when an elephant is very young and continue to grow throughout its life. They can be as long as thirteen feet and weigh as much as 200 pounds." The students continue in this manner until everyone who wants to share has a chance.

After the reading, Ty asks students to share why their selection was important to them. Lupe says, "Thirteen feet and 200 pounds. . . . Those are really big tusks!" Patrick agrees, "I also chose my selection because it had crazy information that I didn't know." There is no shortage on students wanting to tell why the part they selected was their favorite! Ty closes the lesson by saying, "You all learned a lot about elephants! Sharing our favorite parts and reasoning was a really fun and interesting way to show what we learned from our reading."

Terrific Texts for *Listen to Me*

Title	Author (Last, First)	Publisher/Year	ISBN
Elephants of Africa	Gibbons, Gail	Holiday House/2008	9780823421688
Really Truly Bingo	Kvasnosky, Laura	Candlewick/2008	9780763632106
Kitchen Dance	Manning, Maurie	Clarion/2008	9780618991105
I'm Just Like My Mom/ I'm Just Like My Dad: Me parezco tanto a mi mama/Me parezco tantoa mi papa	Ramos, Jorge	HarperCollins/2008	9780061239687
Smile	Rowe, John	Penguin/2008	9780698400887
Skippyjon Jones in Mummy Trouble	Schachner, Judy	Puffin/2006	9780525477549
Kids Like Us	Schaefer, Carole	Viking/2008	9780670062904
Vunce Upon a Time	Seibold, J. Otto Vivian, Siobhan	Chronicle/2008	9780811862714
Up, Up, Up! It's Apple-Picking Time	Shapiro, Jody	Holiday House/2003	9780823416103
My Mei Mei	Young, Ed	Philomel/2006	9780399243394

Winning Websites

www.earlychildhoodlinks.com/teachers/childrensliterature.htm is a website that allows you to surf children's literature databases, guides, and reviews.

www.4children.org/news/9-97mlit.htm provides information on how to select multicultural literature.

www.ala.org/ala/mgrps/divs/alsc/awardsgrants/bookmedia/ index.cfm has ALSC books and media awards with lists including Newbery Medal and Caldecott Medal titles.

Handy Hints

1. One way to extend this activity is to have students summarize what they learned as a result of reading and listening to others. Yet another way to extend the lesson is to have students write their favorite passage in a personalized reading journal. Students might opt to illustrate their passage, too.

2. Create a class book by having students write and illustrate their selected part. Collect them and assemble them into a book.

3. Consider modifying the activity altogether by having students use texts they have read or are reading during independent reading time. They can share the bibliographic information, give a brief overview, and then read a favorite segment. All texts, including those that use more than one language, can be deemed worthy for this reading experience.

Using Oral Reading with Expanding Language Learners (Level 4)

The fourth graders come back from lunch and three expanding ELLs are talking a mile a minute about last night's basketball game. They are using terminology specific to basketball and laughing as they recount some of the events from the game. I (Lindsey) think to myself, "Talking, talking, talking . . . this group of students is always talking to each other about something!" I give the students another moment to finish up their conversations because I am elated to hear the ELLs use English in authentic contexts. Their frequency and accuracy of conversational English has greatly improved since the beginning of the year.

Once they quiet down, I direct their attention to the task at hand for the science lesson: locating and identifying specific facts from the chapter on recycling. I say, "Please review and reread the chapter we read on recycling with a partner, and select the five facts you found most intriguing." I walk around as the students follow these directions and hear the expanding ELLs reading with fluency and selecting five facts with relative ease.

Right before I am about to call them back together, Annie says, "That was a piece of cake!" Valencia and Carla glance at each other with a puzzled look. Valencia says to Annie, "There is no cake. That was a can (referring to the picture of recyclable materials in their text)." Now all three girls look puzzled, so I ask Annie to explain what she means when she says, "That was a piece of cake!" She does and all three girls laugh as Valencia then comments, "Winning the game last night was a piece of cake!"

As seen in this scenario, *expanding ELLs'* everyday language proficiency is adequate for most all daily interactions. They have progressed through the first three levels of proficiency and are feeling more comfortable taking risks with English. Although at this point, everyday interactions with peers may no longer feel like a risk because they are able to communicate effectively with little to no difficulty. Students in the *expanding* level are continuing to increase their ability to comprehend and use academic language. Most students at this level generally read with fluency and accuracy, but may still have difficulty with abstract academic concepts, decontextualized information, and figurative language.

Just like Valencia and Carla, many *expanding ELLs* find figurative language confusing. Thankfully, they felt comfortable enough to ask for clarification. Clearly, some students won't be so brave, so one of the best ways to support their needs is to use purposeful oral reading strategies. Figure 6–1 provides an overview of appropriate oral reading strategies for teachers to use when designing meaningful instruction for *expanding ELLs*.

Reading Skills	Get the Picture	Readers Theatre	Directed Listening Thinking Activity (DLTA)	Find the Facts	What Does It Mean?
Strategies					
Positive Attitudes/Interest in Reading	•	•	•	•	•
Reading Comprehension	•	•		•	•
Listening Comprehension		•	•		
Social Vocabulary		•			
Academic Vocabulary	•	•	•	•	•
Use of Language Cues	•	•		•	
Predicting		•	•		•
Forming Images	•	•	•		
Using Prior Knowledge	•		•		•
Monitoring			•		•
Inferring			•		•
Fluency (R = rate, A = accuracy, P = prosody)		R A P			
Skimming				•	

Figure 6–1. Effective Oral Reading Strategies and Skills for Expanding Language Learners

Get the Picture

Instructional Information

Imaging (Chamot and O'Malley 1994) is a strategy that helps students create a mental image of text to support their comprehension and understanding. The teacher facilitates the initial creation of mental images (also called visualizations, mind movies, pictures in your head) by selecting and reading a text or portion of a text that will assist students in being able to imagine the scene being described. Students can describe or illustrate their mental image of a scene or summary from the teacher-selected passage. The focus on creating and describing mental images allows not only for nonthreatening and authentic uses of English but also for engaging opportunities for interactions and scaffolding surrounding strategy use.

Researchers investigating reading comprehension have reported findings that proficient readers use imaging while poor readers do not (Irwin 1991). Because of these findings, Herrell and Jordan (2008) recommend imaging as one of fifty suggested strategies for teaching ELLs. For *expanding ELLs*, use *Get the Picture* with a variety of text genres to encourage the use of mental imaging to enhance comprehension.

Savvy Suggestions

1. Select a text that provides language to encourage vivid imaging.

2. Tell students that you are going to start with one scene, so you want them to focus on creating a mental image from the short passage you are going to read.

3. Read a short passage.

4. Invite students to sketch on paper the image that they see in their mind. Have students describe their sketches before showing them to a partner and discussing similarities and differences.

5. Read the next short passage.

6. Ask partners to describe and compare their mental image without drawing a sketch.

7. Continue using steps 5 and 6 for the remainder of the activity.

8. Remind students to use imaging in their daily reading because it will help them to comprehend the text and to enjoy it, too.

Classroom Conversations

Understanding the strengths and needs of her *expanding ELLs*, Katey uses her small-group reading time for strategy instruction and practice in her third-grade classroom. This week she decides to teach imaging because she knows it is a strategy that proficient readers use to help with comprehension. *Imagine a Place* (Thomson 2008) is perfect to use with the *Get the Picture* strategy because of its emphasis on imagination and vivid descriptions that lend themselves to mental imagery.

Katey opens the lesson by saying, "Strong readers create mental pictures or movies in their minds as they read. Today we are going to use *Imagine a Place* to help us *Get the Picture* in our minds. I will read you a short passage, and I want you to make a picture in your mind." Katey reads the first page and then asks students to sketch their mental images. Students describe their image to a partner and then compare sketches. She walks around the room to observe and interact with the partners. All the sketches are different and students are describing and comparing. Katey reads the next short passage, "Imagine a place . . . where water is solid, light is liquid, sky a frozen river flowing under your feet." After giving students a moment to visualize, she tells them, "Turn to your partner and describe the picture you created in your head." As she walks around she hears Kareem say, "I see myself walking through clouds like grass on the dark frozen river in the sky." Anastacia replies, "Me too, but I also see the sun turning into drops like rain!" Katey and the third graders continue in this manner until the book is finished and she closes the lesson by saying, "Good readers create mental pictures when they're reading to help them comprehend. Today, you learned how to do that too! We will continue practicing this next time with our partners. Remember that making movies and pictures in your mind is something you can always be doing when you read. The pictures you create should help you understand the story."

Terrific Texts for *Get the Picture*

Title	Author (Last, First)	Publisher/Year	ISBN
You Can, Toucan, Math: Word Problem-Solving Fun	Adler, David	Holiday House/2006	9780823421176
Soup for Breakfast	Brown, Calef	Houghton Mifflin/2008	9780618916412
The Girl Who Drew a Phoenix	Demi	Margaret K. McElderry Books/2008	9781416953470
What's Under the Bed?	Fenton, Joe	Simon & Schuster/2008	9781416949435
Bow Wow Meow Meow: It's Rhyming Cats and Dogs	Florian, Douglas	Harcourt/2003	9780152163952
Wonderful Words	Hopkins, Lee Bennett	Simon & Schuster/2004	9780689835889
A Is for Art: An Abstract Alphabet	Johnson, Stephen T.	Paula Wiseman Books/ 2008	9780689863011
Racer Dogs	Kolar, Bob	Dutton/2003	9780525459392
Punk Wig	Ries, Lori	Boyds Mills Press/2008	9781590784860
Imagine a Place	Thomson, Sarah L.	Atheneum/2008	9781416968023

Winning Websites

www.readwritethink.org/lessons/lesson_view.asp?id=797 includes a lesson using a visualizing strategy to help synthesize information.

**http://primary-school-curriculum.suite101.com/article.cfm
/nonfiction_text_features** provides ideas for using visualization to
teach comparisons and nonfiction text features.

**http://reading.ecb.org/teacher/visualizing/visual_teachingtips
.html** provides great teaching tips for imaging.

Handy Hints

1. Instead of stopping after each passage and asking for a scene
   description, read the entire book. Then, ask students to illustrate
   or describe a mental image they created to summarize the text.

2. Use this strategy with poetry or nonfiction to encourage students
   to visualize new and unfamiliar information.

3. Ask students to describe their mental image using a minimum of
   five adjectives.

4. Imaging can be used across curricular areas including math, science, writing, music, social studies, etc. For example, this strategy
   can be used with word problems during math. Ask the students to
   close their eyes and create a mental picture of the items or objects
   involved in the problem. Students can then describe and solve the
   problem mentally or draw a sketch to illustrate the mental picture
   created from the word problem.

Readers Theatre

Instructional Information

Readers Theatre is a reading activity that helps students use both oral and written language to communicate their understanding and interpretation of a text (Peregoy and Boyle 2008; Black and Stave 2007). In essence, *Readers Theatre* calls on students to read a script to an interested audience; no props are needed. In fact, many times readers often simply sit on stools in front of the audience and read their parts in turn. In addition to providing a relaxed, comfortable atmosphere for *expanding ELLs* to prepare and share with others, *Readers Theatre* helps learners develop many other reading-related skills such as the ability to analyze the story and its characters, how to interpret the story, and how to convey their interpretation to others.

When first using *Readers Theatre*, teachers scaffold students by either developing a script with them or giving them a ready-made script with which to practice. The teacher also scaffolds students' learning by giving them plenty of time to rehearse, which provides all children with language practice. As a result of this practice, the affective filter is low when they do finally perform and they do so with ease.

Once children are familiar and comfortable with *Readers Theatre*, though, Peregoy and Boyle (2008) suggest that to get the most out of the experience, *expanding-level ELLs* are ready and need to go beyond reading, interpreting, and performing premade scripts. The researchers suggest showing students how to create their own scripts, either from an original script they compose or by using a familiar story and turning it into a script. Doing so challenges and affords students with the opportunity to develop further reading and writing skills. Because I offer this strategy as a way of facilitating the reading growth of *expanding-level ELLs,* the teaching suggestions include having children create their own scripts.

Savvy Suggestions

1. Select an appealing text that can be easily turned into a script. You might want to begin with a text in which two different fonts are used to convey two different characters.

2. Read aloud the text to students.

3. Tell students that you would like to turn the text into a script that could be used for *Readers Theatre*. Demonstrate how you identify the characters, what they will say, and how you will record both in a script format.

4. Tell students that they will be following the same process when preparing for their *Readers Theatre* performance.

5. Divide students into groups based on the number of characters in the story, making sure to include ELLs and native English speakers in each group.

6. Assign or have each group select a book from an array of books that you have preselected to ensure their success.

7. Provide time for students to read the text silently and to create their scripts. Provide help as needed.

8. Provide time for students to perform for an interested audience.

Classroom Conversations

John is a big believer in *Readers Theatre*. Past experience has taught him that to be successful with it, students need to use prepared scripts. Once they can use the scripts with ease, he uses what his fifth graders know about *Readers Theatre* to teach them something they have yet to learn: how to turn a book into a script. Today is the day he is going to do just that. In addition to changing up the *Readers Theatre* activity to keep students interested in it, his larger reason for having students create scripts is to deepen their understanding of the text, to comprehend it at a deeper level. He opens the lesson saying, "We have been using *Readers Theatre* quite a bit and it seems to be helping you interpret characters and story events. You seem to be very good at showing others your interpretations when reading your scripts, too. Today we're going to take it a step further. I'm going to show you how to create your own script. After you create it, you can use it to perform for others, just like you do when you use a script that has already been made for you." "You mean we're going to take a story and actually turn it into a play?" asks Juan. "That's exactly right, Juan. There's nothing to be afraid of. I'm going to show you how and help you along the way if you need it." "But why do we have to create our own when you have all of those books that have the scripts already made?" Jamie inquires. "Great question, so let me answer it for you. When you take a text and turn it into a script like this, you have to think a lot more about it. You have to think about the characters and why they act the way they do. You also have to think about how they might sound when talking so that you can help others to understand the characters. In other words, turning a story into a script helps you to become even better readers because it gives you time to really think about all parts of the story. This is the kind of thinking that readers do when they read stories to themselves in order to stay interested in the story and to enjoy it, too."

John then uses *Beware of the Frog* (Bee 2008) and the previously listed steps to demonstrate and support students as they go about to creating their scripts. He is pleased that students asked about the activity because it gave him an opportunity to help students see that deeper understanding is the goal of creating the script rather than the *Readers Theatre* activity.

Terrific Texts for *Readers Theatre*

Title	Author (Last, First)	Publisher/Year	ISBN
Babies in the Bayou	Arnosky, Jim	G.P. Putnam's Sons/2007	9780399226533
Beware of the Frog	Bee, William	Candlewick/2008	9780763639204
Thump, Quack, Moo: A Whacky Adventure	Cronin, Doreen	Atheneum/2008	9781416916307
I Lost My Tooth In Africa	Diakite, Penda	Scholastic/2006	978043966265

Title	Author (Last, First)	Publisher/Year	ISBN
No Hugs Till Saturday	Downing, Julie	Clarion/2008	9780618910786
Lincoln and Douglass: An American Friendship	Giovanni, Nikki	Henry Holt & Company/2008	9780805082647
Mama Mine, Mama Mine	Gray, Rita	Dutton/2008	9780525472063
Winter Waits	Plourde, Lynn	Simon & Schuster/2001	9780689832680
Me Hungry!	Tankard, Jeremy	Candlewick/2008	9780763633608
Chalk & Cheese	Warnes, Tim	Simon & Schuster/2008	9781416913788

Winning Websites

http://scriptsforschools.com offers several free readers theatre scripts for all grades as well as some teaching suggestions for using readers theatre.

http://pbskids.org/zoom/activities/playhouse is one way to connect to ZOOM, a children's PBS television show, with readers theatre. The site features scripts from short plays performed on the show with numerous extension activities.

www.storycart.com provides several free readers theatre scripts as well as those that can be purchased.

Handy Hints

1. Instead of having students write their own scripts, you may wish to provide them with premade scripts. If so, there are numerous scripts from which to select. Use the websites listed to access some of them.

2. *Readers Theatre* is a perfect way to incorporate visualizing. Because no props are used, students are left to their own to imagine how the setting and characters might actually appear. After a

performance, give students a blank piece of paper and have them draw one event from the story or have them draw what they think a given character might look like. Should students share their drawings, you might also want to point out how readers bring their own background to a story in order to get meaning from it and that this is why their pictures of the same object might look different. For example, if drawing a picture of a tree, some students might draw deciduous trees where as others might draw coniferous trees. Getting them to talk about why they drew what they drew would help all to see that readers interpret ideas in different ways.

3. Consider allowing simple props to support ELLs who may need them to help explain or express their ideas to the audience.

Directed Listening Thinking Activity (DLTA)

Instructional Information

Children need to learn how to listen for a variety of purposes if they are to be successful in school; increased ability to listen translates into better academic performance (see Opitz and Zbaracki 2004 for a review of studies). In terms of comprehension alone, there is ample evidence that listening and reading comprehension are connected. That is, those who are able to demonstrate listening comprehension tend to be able to do the same with reading comprehension.

The *DLTA* is one way to help students learn how to listen. It calls on learners to listen to a story and to make predictions before and while the story is being read aloud. Over thirty years ago, Stauffer (1975) reported that the *DLTA* was an effective method for using prior knowledge to improve students' listening comprehension, schema, and thinking skills. Since that time, others have also reported success with using the *DLTA* with ELLs (Diamond and Moore 1995). The *DLTA* is an excellent way to teach students how to listen and to learn more about text structure simultaneously. What's more, it is an excellent way to scaffold *expanding-level ELLs* reading comprehension because students practice the very same comprehension strategy through listening before using it when reading. Using listening first, students can attend to the specific strategy, in this case *making predictions*, without having to decode the text. Once they understand the strategy, they can then apply it when reading, which is a little more difficult because they not only have to use the strategy but read the text, too.

Savvy Suggestions *(based on Stauffer 1975)*

1. Select and preview the text you want to share with students. It should be a text that relates to other content that students are learning so that they can see how thinking and making predictions tie into all content areas.

2. Connect the text with students' lives. Ask them to think about what they already know about the topic at hand. Have them make some predictions based on the title and cover illustration.

3. Establish a purpose for listening.

4. Read the text aloud while students actively listen. Stop at designated points to either confirm or change their predictions and to make predictions for the next text segment.

5. Continue reading to the next stopping point and again stop to confirm, modify, question, and form new predictions.

6. Have students summarize the text in some way. This can be an oral summary, an illustration, or a written statement.

7. Remind students that thinking and making predictions are necessary for understanding a text when they are listening and reading.

Classroom Conversations

Rachel decides to use *Follow the Line Around the World* (Ljungkvist 2008) when constructing a *DLTA* for her fourth graders. She sees this as a perfect book to ease students into reading more about the same topics in their social studies textbook. She has used the *DLTA* before and has seen for herself that it really does help all students, especially ELLs and others who strive to be better readers. To prepare for this experience, she has displayed a large world map. She will have student volunteers point to places they are from or have visited that are mentioned in the text at some point in the lesson. She begins by establishing a purpose for listening, "We are going to be learning more about different continents and countries this year and this book is a perfect way to begin. By following the line, we will take an imaginary trip to different places. Take a look at the map. You'll probably recognize some of these places because some of you are from them or have visited them." She then provides volunteers time to point to the countries they recognize. She continues, "By looking at the cover of this book, what are some places you think we might visit? What do you think we will see at each stop? Think and then share your idea with the person next to you." Once partners have shared, Rachel asks for volunteers to share with the group.

"We think we are going to visit Africa because the cover of the book shows it. We think that we'll probably see a giraffe because it is also on the cover," Richard shares.

"We think that we are going to visit Australia because there is a rabbit on the cover. There are rabbits in Australia, aren't there?" asks Autumn.

Sharing completed, Rachel continues with the lesson by beginning reading aloud. When she finishes reading, "Turn the page and feel the hot sun in . . ." she stops and asks students to think of a place that has a lot of sun and to use their thinking to make a prediction. After providing students some time to share their predictions with one another, she turns the page and asks, "Were you correct? Where is Kenya?" Rachel continues in like manner throughout the remainder of the text. To bring the lesson to a close, Rachel first encourages volunteers to put a pushpin on every continent that was mentioned in the text as a way to summarize the text. She then states, "You did a lot of thinking and you made several accurate predictions. This shows that you understood the story. You can do the same when you are reading to yourself. Thinking and making predictions before and during reading help you to understand what you are reading."

Terrific Texts for *DLTA*

Title	Author (Last, First)	Publisher/Year	ISBN
The Umbrella Queen	Bridges, Shirin	Greenwillow/2008	9780060750411
Walking to School	Bunting, Eve	Clarion/2008	9780618261444
Horse	Doyle, Malachy	Margaret K. McElderry Books/2008	9780689835032
Bees, Snails, and Peacock Tails	Franco, Betsy	Margaret K. McElderry Books/2008	9781416903864
A Home for Dixie	Jackson, Emma	HarperCollins/2008	9780061449635
The Paper Princess Flies Again: With Her Dog!	Kleven, Elisa	Tricycle/2005	9781582461465
Follow the Line Around the World	Ljungkvist, Laura	Viking/2008	9780670063345
My Friend, the Starfinder	Lyon, George	Atheneum/2008	9781416927389
Cat Nights	Manning, Jane	Greenwillow/2008	9780061138898
For the Love of Autumn	Polacco, Patricia	Philomel/2008	9780399245411

Winning Websites

www.readwritethink.org/lessons/lesson_view.asp?id=850 provides a DLTA for the text "The Tell-Tale Heart" by Edgar Allan Poe. The lesson can be adapted to suit other texts.

http://thelife.com/students/people/listen/?request_uri=/people/listen.html contains ten tips for helping students to become active listeners. Taken together, the tips can be displayed on a chart as each tip is taught and practiced.

www.lessonplanet.com offers teacher-created lessons on many different topics including making predictions. Lessons for many different grade levels are provided for each topic.

Handy Hints

1. *Sneak Preview* (DeHaven 1989) is another way to use the basic *DLTA* elements. Using this activity, though, after stopping at designated points, students draw what they think will happen in the succeeding text segment. Students share their pictures with a partner and state what led them to think that what they drew might happen next. As with the original *DLTA*, the reading continues and students continue to make and modify predictions as necessary.

2. *Expanding-level ELLs* sometimes need additional help with understanding grade-level content vocabulary. One way to help them is to use a modified version of the *DLTA* in which the teacher gives or invites students to make some questions about the text to be read. The teacher then reads the section while students listen. At the end of the section, students look through their questions and indicate which were addressed. This procedure is appropriate for nearly every content area.

Find the Facts

Instructional Information

Adjusting reading rate to the purpose for reading is one of many proficient reader behaviors (Kucer 2005). *Expanding ELLs* are able to read with fluency (i.e., rate, accuracy, and prosody) and are able to identify facts within a text. However, they, along with many other children, often need some help in understanding that reading rate is dependent on one's purpose for reading. What children need to understand is that readers speed up and slow down within and across a variety of texts to show their interpretation and understanding of the texts and that doing so is natural (Flurkey 2006). *Find the Facts* is designed to help them learn just that. It emphasizes teaching students how to use skimming to locate specific information. Because ELLs at this *expanding level* are already able to identify facts, when using *Find the Facts* teachers are using something students know to teach them something they need to learn. They are teaching from the known to the unknown and in so doing, are making the learning meaningful and less arduous. While this activity can be used with the whole class, it is better suited to a small-group activity. The best-case scenario is to begin with the whole class, break out into small groups, and then come back together as a whole class.

Savvy Suggestions

1. Select a text or texts for students to read. Select texts that have a common topic.

2. Explain the term *skimming* by saying something like this: "Readers always have a purpose for reading a text. Sometimes they read to find some specific information, kind of like when you are looking for something on a website to share with someone else or to find an answer to a question you might have. To find the specific information they are looking for, readers read pretty quickly and

they do not read every word. Instead, they use a technique called *skimming*."

3. Demonstrate how to skim using one of the selected texts that students will also use.

4. Explain the procedure for reading the texts, demonstrating each step. See Figure 6–2 for a sample.

5. Provide time for students to silently read and to share information.

6. Conclude the lesson by emphasizing that knowing the purpose for reading, in this case to locate specific facts, is what helps readers determine their reading speed. Emphasize that while skimming was useful for this particular activity, it would be inappropriate for reading mathematics problems or poetry.

Classroom Conversations

Sasha's observations of his third graders have helped him to see that they enjoy learning about dinosaurs. His observations have also helped him to see that students need to learn how to adjust their rate of reading to their purpose for reading. He decides to use their interest to his best advantage. He gathers several texts about dinosaurs such as *Dinosaurs!* (Gibbons 2008) and *Boy, Were We Wrong About Dinosaurs!*

---

1. Select one text from the center of the table.

2. Within two minutes, look through the text and locate one fact that you finding interesting.

3. Remember that you read quickly when skimming because you do not need to read every word. You are looking for specific information instead.

4. When I call time, please stop your reading.

5. Share the fact that you identified.

6. Pass your text to the person on your right and repeat steps 2–5.

Figure 6–2. Skimming Procedures

(Kudlinski 2005) to teach students how to skim to locate specific information and how to adjust reading speed for the purpose of skimming. He will also integrate this lesson with his animal unit in science.

He begins the lesson with the whole class by telling them he's noticed that they read books about dinosaurs during their independent reading time. He continues by asking questions such as, "So when you read these books, what do you do? Do you read every page? Do you look at the pictures? Do you read it in order or do you skip around?" Students are quick to provide insights. "Tyrannosaurus Rex is my favorite dinosaur so when I read dinosaur books, I look for information about him. I also look at the illustrations," shares Pablo. "I do the same thing," says Mary. She continues, "It saves me a lot of time. But stegosaurus is my favorite dinosaur."

After listening to several volunteer responses, Sasha capitalizes on their comments by stating, "So books can be read in many different ways. Today I want to focus on something you seem to sometimes do without realizing it. When you glance at pictures or look through your text to find specific information, you are *skimming*. Skimming is very helpful for readers because it saves much time and helps them identify what they want to know. This is a skill we use when we are looking for specific information. Any time you skim read, you read quickly because you are looking for specific information. You don't need to read all of the words. Quick reading and skimming are a good fit. We're going to practice *skimming* during small-group reading today using these dinosaur books." One by one, he displays the books.

The lesson continues with Sasha teaching students in small groups of five. A pile of the six dinosaur books he previously shared with the whole class is in the center of the table. After students are settled, Sasha provides them with directions using an overhead transparency that shows the directions shown in Figure 6–2. He models each step as he states it and then provides students with time to select their books and to complete the skimming. Once all groups have met with him, Sasha gathers the whole class together to conclude the lesson. He comments, "Skimming is an important way to read when you are trying to locate a specific idea or piece of information. Knowing your purpose for reading helps you to know how to set the correct pace for reading it."

Terrific Texts for *Find the Facts*

Title	Author (Last, First)	Publisher/Year	ISBN
Young Thomas Edison	Dooling, Michael	Holiday House/2005	9780823418688
Dinosaurs!	Gibbons, Gail	Holiday House/2008	9780823421978
How Many Ways Can You Catch a Fly?	Jenkins, Steve Page, Robin	Houghton Mifflin/2008	9780618966349
Wind Flyers	Johnson, Angela	Simon & Schuster/2007	9780689848797
A Man for All Seasons: The Life of George Washington Carver	Krensky, Stephen	Amistad/2008	9780060278861
Boy, Were We Wrong About Dinosaurs!	Kudlinski, Kathleen	Puffin/2005	9781845079079
A Voice of Her Own: The Story of Phillis Weatley, Slave Poet	Lasky, Kathryn	Candlewick/2003	9780763628789
Mr. Lincoln's Boys	Rabin, Staton	Viking/2008	9780670061693
Like People	Schubert, Ingrid Schubert, Dieter	Lemniscaat/2008	9781590785768
Sandy's Circus: A Story About Alexander Calder	Stone, Tanya	Viking/2008	9780670062683

Winning Websites

www.enchantedlearning.com/subjects/dinosaurs/ offers a wealth of information about dinosaurs including fact sheets for numerous dinosaurs that are a perfect fit for *Find the Facts*.

www.timeforkids.com provides several reading comprehension lessons that coincide with *Time for Kids* magazines. Reading for information is one such lesson.

www.sciencenewsforkids.org is a gold mine for science topics of interest to kids. Additional texts, including Web resources, are also provided.

Handy Hints

1. Using available content-area textbooks is one way to connect this activity with something students are learning in a given content area such as social studies. After previewing a given chapter with students in which you call attention to the subheadings, instruct students to select one heading and the text that follows it and skim to locate a fact to share with others.

2. Most children enjoy reading magazines such as *Zoobooks*. Use magazines to complete the very same skimming activity. In fact, just about any genre can be used. Students can use joke books, for example, skimming to find a specific joke they want to share with others. Texts such as *How Many Ways Can You Catch a Fly?* (Jenkins and Page 2008) lend themselves to this activity because of the way the text is written.

3. In addition to sharing orally, prepare a note-taking guide in which students can record the facts that they learn by reading and listening to others. They can then take their "fact sheets" home to share information with interested others.

What Does It Mean?

Instructional Information

Comprehension can become more difficult when authors use idioms and figurative language that students may not know (Edwards 1975). These English expressions can be tricky for all learners, but especially for ELLs because they attempt to translate the expression directly into their first language. When reading books such as *Amelia Bedelia Talks Turkey* (Parish 2008) for example, interpreting idioms literally can cause confusion, misunderstandings, and ultimately the breakdown of comprehension. Fortunately, some researchers have documented that figurative language instruction is a necessary component of instruction for ELLs and that it can be taught and learned (Palmer and Brooks 2004). *What Does It Mean?* focuses specifically on helping students understand idioms, but the activity can easily be adapted to address other types of figurative language.

Providing instruction and activities to support the understanding of idioms with ELLs is widespread (May 1979; Chen and Mora-Flores 2006; Peregoy and Boyle 2008; Vogt and Echevarria 2008). Idioms can be addressed as they arise naturally during instruction, during conversations, or when reading texts that contain them. However, *expanding ELLs* can greatly benefit from teachers calling explicit attention to different idioms, discussing their literal and figurate meanings, and giving students plenty of opportunities to read and use them in authentic contexts. Idiom instruction can be a humorous and entertaining way to help ELLs at the *expanding* level become more proficient readers. As a result of understanding idioms, students are more likely to understand what they read.

Savvy Suggestions

1. Select a book that contains idioms.

2. Read the selected text aloud, and stop after the first idiom.

3. Invite students to turn and talk about the literal and intended meaning for the idiom.

4. Have a volunteer share his or her thoughts while you model the first idiom dictionary entry on an overhead transparency or whiteboard.

5. Have students use a spiral notebook, section of a notebook, stapled or bound papers to make an idiom dictionary template. See an example entry in Figure 6–3.

6. Tell students that you will be using this dictionary to identify idioms, their literal meaning, and their intended meaning. Note that they will also provide a sketch for both the literal and intended meanings.

7. Give students time to copy their first entry into their idiom dictionary.

8. Repeat in like manner throughout the text or until you feel students can work in small groups or partners without your guidance.

Idiom	Literal Meaning	Intended Meaning
Raining cats and dog	Cats and dogs are falling out of clouds in the sky.	Raining heavily

Figure 6–3. Sample Idiom Dictionary Entry

9. Explain that while they will discover, learn, and add several idioms to the idiom dictionaries during *What Does It Mean?*, they will also add new entries to their idiom dictionary as they encounter them when reading independently or when talking with others.

Classroom Conversations

After seeing his third-grade *expanding ELL*, Rosa, read *Amelia Bedelia Talks Turkey* (Parish 2008) with a confused look on her face and without cracking a smile, Christopher decided to provide some explicit instruction on idioms. He thinks that *Raining Cats and Dogs* (Moses 2008) is a great introductory text for *What Does It Mean?* because the entire book consists of idioms, their meanings, and entertaining illustrations.

Christopher opens the lesson by showing the cover and reading the title, *Raining Cats and Dogs.* He says, "Look at this cover illustration where cats and dogs are falling from the raining sky! Does this picture show what people really mean when they say 'It's raining cats and dogs'? Describe what you think they really mean. Turn and talk to someone next to you." As volunteers share their ideas and clarify the meaning of the idiom, Christopher uses an overhead transparency of the idiom dictionary template to fill in the new idiom and illustrations to accompany the literal and intended meaning. Miguel shouts, "You're crazy! It can't rain cats and dogs. I guess I don't know exactly what it means, but I know it doesn't really mean that cats and dogs come out of the sky!" Vanessa clarifies, "Yeah. I think it means that it is raining really hard." Christopher chuckles and replies, "Both of you are correct. Idioms are expressions we use to explain something that is happening." Christopher continues the lesson by telling students that they will be learning and discovering other idioms and that they will create an idiom dictionary to keep track of them. Christopher then passes out copies of stapled packets for their idiom dictionaries. Inside the packets are blank templates similar to Figure 6–3 for the students to write their entries. Christopher says, "If you open up your new idiom dictionary you will see that, just like on the example I shared with you using the overhead, there is a box for you to write each new idiom. Next to each idiom box, there are boxes to put the literal meaning and intended meaning with illustrations. Let's try 'Raining cats and dogs' for your first entry." He gives time for students to complete their first idiom entry. They continue on in a like manner completing entries for the first five idioms in the book. Christopher closes the lesson by saying, "Today we learned about idioms and how their literal and intended meanings are often quite different. This can be tricky for readers, but we are going to continue *What Does It Mean?* in small groups throughout the week because understanding idioms will also help you to understand what you read. We'll add to your idiom dictionaries but you can keep them so that any time you find one, you can add it to your dictionary."

Terrific Texts for *What Does It Mean?*

Title	Author (Last, First)	Publisher/Year	ISBN
My Teacher Likes to Say	Brennan-Nelson, Denise	Sleeping Bear Press/2004	9781585362127
The Fish Who Cried Wolf	Donaldson, Julia	Arthur A. Levine Books/2007	9780545034548
Americana Adventure	Garland, Michael	Dutton/2008	9780525479451
Flyboy of Underwhere	Hale, Bruce	HarperCollins/2008	9780060851316
Ellen's Apple Tree	Kruusval, Catarina	R & S Books/2008	9789129669053
Crazy Like a Fox: A Simile Story	Leedy, Loreen	Holiday House/2008	9780823417193
Raining Cats and Dogs	Moses, Will	Philomel/2008	9780399242335
Come Back, Cat	Nodset, Joan	HarperCollins/2008	9780060280819
Amelia Bedelia Talks Turkey	Parish, Herman	Greenwillow/2008	9780060843526
Scarecrow	Rylant, Cynthia	Harcourt Brace & Company/1998	9780152010843

Winning Websites

www.idiomconnection.com provides idioms organized both alpha-betically and by topic. It also denotes the eighty most common idiomatic expressions.

www.rong-chang.com/idioms.htm contains links to many different idiom websites.

http://english-zone.com/index.php has an idiom zone including those for animals, the body, food, relationships, and a dictionary of idioms.

Handy Hints

1. Have students create a class idiom book. Each student or set of partners can find one or two idioms to write, define, and illustrate. Once all class members have completed their idiom(s), they can be published in a class book, which can become a book in the class-room library.

2. Many cultures and languages have idioms (see, for example, the children's book *Ve lo que dices/See What You Say* [Tabor 2000]). Ask students to talk with their family and friends to try to find new idioms from other cultures or languages. These new idioms can be entered into their idiom dictionary or be used to create a new class idiom book.

3. Create an idiom game for ELLs to practice their understanding of idioms. Create a memory-like game and write the idiom and its intended meaning on two separate index cards. Mix up idiom and intended meaning cards and place them in a folder. Students can place the cards face down (so the text is not showing) and play memory using the correct idiom and intended meaning as a match/pair.

4. The suggested titles in this chapter include books with figurative language and are not necessarily specific to idioms. Adapt this strategy to use with other types of figurative language such as similes and metaphors.

Using Oral Reading with Bridging Language Learners (Level 5)

As I listen to my second-grade son and his Korean friend discuss a book they are reading at school, I (Michael) marvel at how well Woo Jae uses English. He has no problem getting his ideas across or debating those posed by Josh. I can't help but think that if I were not in the room and was listening without seeing them, I would have no idea that Woo Jae was from Korea and that he can and does speak both Korean and English with ease. How is he able to do this? He's only been in the United States for two years. Curiosity gets the best of me and so I decide to ask him. He tells me that he has been going to Saturday English school while in the United States, but that he started learning English when he was in Korea. In reflecting on how Woo Jae uses English both for conversational and academic purposes, I realize that even though he is only eight years old, he is exhibiting characteristics fitting of a "bridging language learner."

Like Woo Jae, *bridging language learners* are characterized by their ability to use English with few difficulties. They understand idioms, possess and use both conversational and academic vocabulary, and can use both when needed with little to no support. In short, they have now surpassed their English-only counterparts. After all, they now know and use more than one language.

Although they have a good command of English and have little difficulty reading, these learners are like many other learners; they may need some help in developing more sophisticated reading and thinking skills. The oral reading strategies this chapter showcases provide this support. Figure 7–1 provides an overview of the strategies and the skills they are designed to develop and elicit.

Reading Skills	Directed Reading Thinking Activity (DRTA)	Response Quad	Follow the Guide	Poetry Circle	Let's Get Critical
Strategies					
Positive Attitudes/Interest in Reading	•	•	•	•	•
Reading Comprehension	•	•	•	•	•
Listening Comprehension		•		•	•
Social Vocabulary		•		•	•
Academic Vocabulary	•	•	•		•
Use of Language Cues		•	•	•	
Predicting	•		•		•
Forming Images				•	
Using Prior Knowledge	•				•
Monitoring	•	•	•		
Inferring	•		•	•	•
Fluency (R = rate, A = accuracy, P = prosody)		R A P		R A P	
Skimming			•		

Figure 7–1. Effective Oral Reading Strategies and Skills for Bridging Language Learners

Directed Reading Thinking Activity (DRTA)

Instructional Information

Even students at the *bridging* level, who can express themselves fluently in both everyday and academic settings, may need practice with making predictions as they read. *Directed Reading Thinking Activity (DRTA)* is a strategy that boosts reading comprehension by making transparent how proficient readers make and confirm predictions while they read (Diaz-Rico 2008). Similar to the *DLTA* found in the previous chapter, Stauffer (1975) reported that *DRTA* was an effective method for using prior knowledge to improve reading comprehension, schema, and thinking skills. The *DRTA* is facilitated by teacher support before, during, and after reading to provide a model of active questioning that students will eventually be able to carry out independently without teacher scaffolding (Peregoy and Boyle 2008).

The *DRTA* is a great activity to help teach reading for meaning. It is carried out in the same manner as the *DLTA* except students read the text to themselves instead of listening *to it*. Because of the increased proficiency at the *bridging* level, these ELLs are ready for a more challenging activity in which they have to focus on the strategy, *making predictions*, and simultaneously read the text.

Savvy Suggestions *(based on Stauffer 1975)*

1. Select the text you want the students to read. While previewing the text, make note of logical stopping points for the readers to make predictions and have discussions.

2. Discuss and activate students' schema related to the topic or book that they are going to read.

3. Ask students to make predictions based on the title and cover illustration.

4. Establish a purpose for reading.

5. Have students read the text that you have selected. Be specific by giving students a designated stopping point to confirm or change their predictions and make predictions for the next text segment.

6. Discuss their confirmations, modifications, and new predictions for the next text selection as a class before giving them the next stopping point. Continue in this manner.

7. Have students summarize the text in some way. This can be an oral summary, an illustration, or a written statement.

8. Remind students that thinking and making predictions are necessary for understanding a text when they are reading.

Classroom Conversations

Holly selects *Chee-Lin: A Giraffe's Journey* (Rumford 2008) for a *DRTA* she designs for her fifth graders. She thinks *Chee-Lin*, a story based on the life of a real giraffe's travels from Africa to Bengal to China, will be an ideal text because of its logical connection to their world geography unit and naturally occurring stopping points of storybook chapters. Knowing that *bridging ELLs* have a strong command over technical and academic vocabulary, Holly wants to focus on helping students acquire and use reading comprehension strategies independently during their reading. The strategy focus she envisions being most beneficial today is *making predictions*. In preparation for the lesson, she makes copies of world maps for each student. Students will be using the map to document Chee-Lin's travels and the people he meets along his journey. To activate schema and establish a purpose for reading she says, "We have been studying world geography and how to read maps, so this book will be a great way to use what we already know to help our comprehension when reading about Chee-Lin's journey. Judging by the title and cover illustration, what do you think this story will be about? Take a moment to think about it and share your ideas with your partner." Once partners have shared, Holly asks for volunteers.

Andres shares, "I think it will be about a giraffe that travels around the world in a circus."

"I think it will be about a giraffe's journey to find his home because the title says it is about a giraffe's journey," says Amina.

Holly responds by asking students, "Where do you think Chee-Lin will go on his journey? Sketch the route you think Chee-Lin will take using dashed lines with their pencil. Make sure to add the dashed line to a key at the bottom and label it *initial predicted route*."

Holly asks for volunteers to come to the map displayed on the overhead transparency and share their predicted route with the class. Manuel comes to the overhead and explains, "Well, I think the giraffe will start in Asia and then end up somewhere crazy like Antarctica." He sketches his route on the overhead using dashed lines, and Holly calls on the next volunteer to share their predictions.

After the sharing, Holly asks students to read the first page, which reveals that the Chinese found Chee-Lin in Africa. She asks students, "Were you correct? Did you have Chee-Lin's journey starting in Africa? Africa is a big continent; think about where in Africa you want to start your second predicted route." She asks students to use a blue-colored pencil to start a new predicted route for Chee-Lin and reminds them to add the new color to the key and mark it *second predicted route*. Holly continues in this manner throughout the first ten pages. In closing, Holly encourages volunteers to help her review Chee-Lin's journey to this point. She then says, "Today you did a lot of thinking, reading, predicting, and checking predictions. Analyzing your predicted routes and changing them to fit the story shows that you were comprehending what you were reading. You can make predictions before and during your independent reading to help you better understand the text."

Terrific Texts for *DRTA*

Title	Author (Last, First)	Publisher/Year	ISBN
The Moon over Star	Aston, Dianna	Dial/2008	9780803731073
Pirates of the Underwhere	Hale, Bruce	HarperCollins/2008	9780060851286
Bird Lake Moon	Henkes, Kevin	Greenwillow/2008	9780061470769

Title	Author (Last, First)	Publisher/Year	ISBN
Seekers: The Quest Begins	Hunter, Erin	HarperCollins/2008	9780060871222
Night of the Moon	Khan, Hena	Chronicle/2008	9780811860628
The Dragon Tree	Langton, Jane	HarperCollins/2008	9780060823412
The Mystery of the Martello Tower	Lanthier, Jennifer	Laura Geringer Books/ 2006	9780061257124
T4	LeZotte, Anne	Houghton Mifflin/2008	9780547046846
Rosa, Sola	Martino, Carmela	Candlewick/2005	9780763623951
Chee-Lin: A Giraffe's Journey	Rumford, James	Houghton Mifflin/2008	9780618717200

Winning Websites

http://teachers.net/lessonplans/posts/2259.html provides a *DRTA* lesson plan using work of Edgar Allan Poe.

www.philtulga.com/Prediction.html has a prediction game certain to entice students.

www.greece.k12.ny.us/instruction/ela/6-12/tools/index.htm includes a graphic organizer for making predictions, revisiting, and modifying them.

Handy Hints

1. The *DRTA* was traditionally used with narrative texts. However, Peregoy and Boyle (2008) recommend that *DRTA* be used with expository texts. Teachers can model how to make predictions using headings and bold or italicized print.

2. *DRTA* can also be done in small groups or with partners. Students read the selected text to themselves seated with others in small groups or with partners before discussing their predictions, confirmations, and modifications. After the discussion, the students can vote on the most likely prediction from the group and use that to share out and discuss with the entire class.

Response Quad

Instructional Information

Effective teachers motivate students by encouraging participation in classroom discussions and welcoming and valuing their contributions (Cazden 2001; Stipek 2002). Unfortunately, researchers who have conducted research with ELLs as participants report that educators allow ELLs to participate much less than proficient English students (Penfield 1987; Schinke-Llano 1983; Wilhelm, Contreras, and Mohr 2004), and that the majority of interactions include an Initiation-Response-Evaluation (IRE) exchange (Mehan 1979). The IRE may prove difficult for ELLs because they are sometimes unable to articulate the answer in a teacher-expected response (Fitzgerald 1993; Jímenez, Garcia, and Pearson 1996). The *Response Quad* provides opportunities to engage with peers using various language domains to demonstrate their knowledge in an alternative way.

Each of TESOL's (2006) five language proficiency standards is separated into the four language domains of listening, speaking, reading, and writing. The *Response Quad* activity can be used across all curricular areas and utilizes all four language domains. Incorporating individual responsibilities of reading, listening, writing, or speaking during group work enables *bridging ELLs* to use both conversational and academic language to provide valuable contributions that enrich discussions.

Savvy Suggestions *(adapted from Vogt and Echevarria 2008)*

1. Select a text that can be divided into sections or texts on related topics for students to read.

2. Assign each student to a response quad and designate or allow students to select the responsibility of being the reader, listener, writer, or speaker.

3. Explain to students that their group will be the only group reading this material, so it is essential that they work together to synthesize the information and present it to the rest of the class in a meaningful manner.

4. Ask a group to volunteer to help you model how the *Response Quad* process works. Ask the reader to read the first paragraph. Model being the listener and summarize one or two main points from the paragraph. Then, ask group members if they agree. If they do, repeat the main ideas again so that the writer can record them on a sheet of paper. Ask the speaker to read what the writer wrote.

5. Explain to the students that the speaker will present the summary created by the group to the class when they have finished this process with their entire section.

6. Provide time for students to work in their response quads.

7. Once all groups are ready, ask the speakers to share the information with the class.

8. Conclude the lesson by emphasizing how all group members and language domains contributed to comprehending the information in the text and sharing it will the class.

Classroom Conversations

As a way to incorporate group work involving reading, listening, writing, and speaking, Susan decides to have students participate in a *Response Quad*. She has noticed how much her third graders love to learn about other cultures and traditions around the world. Using this knowledge, she purposefully selects the book *How Much? Visiting Markets Around the World* (Lewin 2006). She then divides the group into heterogeneous response quads and tells students that they need to select their role of reader, listener, writer, or speaker.

Once students have agreed on their roles, Susan says, "I know how much you love to learn about other cultures and traditions around the world, so today we are going to learn about different markets around the world! Each group is going to read about a market in a different country, and they will be the only group that reads that section. It is very important that the groups work together to come up with the most important information to share because we all want to learn about markets in other countries." She asks if one group would be willing to help her model what happens in *Response Quad*. The Bangkok group volunteers, and Blake reads the first paragraph. Susan summarizes that Bangkok has a floating market located in small canals, and then she checks with the group to see if they agree. Maria disagrees, "You forgot to say that people shop in boats, and most of the people paddling boats were women!" After discussing it with the group, they decide to have Carrie write down "Bangkok has a floating market where people shop in boats. Most of the people who paddle the boats are women." Maria then reads it aloud to the class.

After giving students ample time to read, listen, and summarize, write and practice speaking, Susan calls the students back together to share out as a class. Each group shares what they learned about markets in their designated country, and the students seem fascinated by the differences. Susan closes the lesson by reminding students, "Wow! Look at how you all worked together to learn new information, share it with the group, and learn from other groups. Today you discussed your reading and important information in your group using reading, listening, writing, and speaking. Isn't it fun to learn new things, talk and work with friends, and use reading, listening, writing, and speaking to share information that *you* think is most important?"

Terrific Texts for *Response Quad*

Title	Author (Last, First)	Publisher/Year	ISBN
Beauty and the Beaks: A Turkey's Cautionary Tale	Auch, Mary Jane	Holiday House/2007	9780823419906
The Book of Wizards	Hague, Michael	HarperCollins/2008	9780688140052
Waggit's Tale	Howe, Peter	HarperCollins/2008	9780061242618
How Much? Visiting Markets Around the World	Lewin, Ted	HarperCollins/2006	9780688175528
Sharks	McMillan, Beverly Music, John	Simon & Schuster/2008	9781416938675
Outcast	Paver, Michelle	HarperCollins/2008	9781842551738
All About Sleep from A to Zzzz	Scott, Elaine	Viking/2008	9780670061884

Title	Author (Last, First)	Publisher/Year	ISBN
Insects & Spiders	Tait, Noel	Simon & Schuster/2008	9781416938682
The Dove Dove: Funny Homograph Riddles	Terban, Marvin	Clarion/2008	9780899198101
Meow: Cat Stories from Around the World	Yolen, Jane	HarperCollins/2005	9780060291617

Winning Websites

www.tefllogue.com/in-the-classroom/jigsaw-activities.html includes jigsaw activities and cooperative vocabulary games and activities.

www.pgcps.pg.k12.md.us/~elc/learning1.html provides various cooperative learning techniques and a rationale for using each.

www.gdrc.org/kmgmt/c-learn/methods.html includes collaborative learning structures and techniques.

Handy Hints

1. For younger ELLs, adapt the *Response Quad* strategy by having students read and write a smaller amount of text. For example, have them read one paragraph of a story and instead of writing the main points, have them create an illustration. The speakers can then use the illustration as they orally summarize the story.

2. In order to ensure that all students have the opportunity to experience each responsibility, think about changing the roles after every paragraph. Create role cards with the title of the role on each card (*reader, listener, writer, speaker*), and instruct students to rotate the role cards clockwise after each paragraph. When it is time to share with the class, give each student in turn an opportunity to share what the group wrote.

Follow the Guide

Instructional Information

As with many children who encounter expository text when reading their textbooks, *bridging-level ELLs* need some help in navigating it (Vacca and Vacca 2008). Even though they are able to use academic vocabulary, expository text is written using many different text structures, some of which students need to learn in order to best comprehend the text. Another problem many students face when reading textbooks centers on reading stamina. They have to be able to stay focused for long periods of time, and they need to be able to tease out major ideas during these long stretches. One way that teachers can scaffold students is to provide students with some sort of reading guide.

While there are many types of reading guides (Wood, Flood, Lapp, and Taylor 2007), *Follow the Guide* capitalizes on the selective reading guide (Cunningham and Shablak 1975). This type of guide helps students glean important information from a content textbook chapter and helps them learn how to adjust reading rate to their purpose for reading.

Using a selective reading guide requires some forethought. Teachers need to think through the text students will be reading and make some decisions about what it is they want students to take away from the reading experience. Teachers must take into consideration their students' background knowledge for the topic at hand. They then construct a guide for students to use when reading. In order for students to be successful in using the guide, however, *Follow the Guide* calls on the teacher to first read some sections of the text, all the while demonstrating how to use the guide. Once students understand how to use the guide, the teacher shifts more of the learning onto students' shoulders by having them use it independently and providing evidence that they did indeed use the guide as intended. Keep in mind that, just as with the other activities in this book, when students no longer need this type of scaffolding, it needs to be removed. The goal is to help students become hooked on reading rather than on the activities themselves.

Savvy Suggestions

1. Read the text students will be reading and ask yourself these questions: "What is it that students need to know when they are finished reading this particular chapter? What background information do students need in order to understand the ideas that I want them to learn from this chapter?"

2. Read the chapter and identify the information you want students to attain.

3. Select only those sections for students to read that will enable them to acquire the information you have identified as being essential.

4. Construct a guide that directs students to the parts they need to read. See Figure 7–2 for an example.

Reading Directions/Questions	Your Ideas
1. Read to page 6, paragraph 1. The author says that America had some rules. What were they called? Did they work as intended?	
2. Page 9, paragraph 2: What does it mean to be "a small man of great learning"? Who is the author talking about?	
3. Page 10, paragraph 2: Why does the author say that people were so happy to see George Washington? Do you agree with her ideas?	

Figure 7–2. Selective Reading Guide for *We the People* (Cheney 2008)

5. Explain the purpose for the reading guide and demonstrate how to use it.

6. Once students show an understanding of how to use the guide, have them use it independently.

7. Using their guides and information they have gleaned, invite students to discuss their findings. If you do some sort of brainstorming activity before students read, compare their findings with what they stated during the initial brainstorming activity.

Classroom Conversations

Sol knows that his fourth-grade students will be learning about the Constitution in social studies. He also knows that most students, *bridging ELLs* included, will need some help sifting through the textbook chapter to get the main ideas. He's also been encouraging them to adjust their reading rate to their purpose for reading. To that end, he has been teaching students how to skim to locate specific information. He sees that the *Follow the Guide* strategy will enable him to scaffold students' learning because it will enable students to use what they already know about adjusting reading rate to the purpose for reading. He will also scaffold their learning by modeling the reading guide using *We the People* (Cheney 2008), which focuses on some of the very content they will be reading in their textbooks. Having followed the teaching suggestions listed previously, he is ready to demonstrate how to use a selective reading guide. Sol first generates interest in the text by giving students some time to talk about what they already know about the Constitution saying, "You all know that the United States is governed by the Constitution but what else do you know about it?" As students share their ideas, he writes them on the board. He will return to their ideas later on once students have had some time to learn more about the Constitution.

Sol continues the lesson by letting students in on a new idea he has discovered that is designed to help them read their textbook. He comments, "You know that we have been working on understanding how to adjust our reading rate to our purpose for reading and you have been doing a very good job of using what you know. Sometimes, though, the authors provide so much information that we can have a hard time finding what it is we want to know. That's where a reading guide and your teacher come in handy! Take this book, for example. I have already read it thinking about you as readers and what I think you should know. I designed this guide to help you focus only on the information that I want you to pay attention to when you are reading. Once you have used the guide, we'll discuss what you have discovered. I think you'll see that this guide will help you to comprehend yet it will also help you read the material more quickly. Let me show you how it works."

Sol then displays the reading guide for *We the People* on an overhead transparency and demonstrates how to use it. He then invites students to participate by having them listen to the next part of the text as identified on the guide and having them share what they discovered. Once he sees that students understand how to use the guide, he closes the lesson saying, "It looks like you understand how to use this guide when listening to me read. You are going to do the same thing with your textbook but instead of listening to me, you are going to read it yourselves." Sol shares the guide he has created for their social studies chapter that has information about the Constitution and provides time for students to read and respond helping those who need additional assistance.

Terrific Texts for *Follow the Guide*

Title	Author (Last, First)	Publisher/Year	ISBN
Celia Cruz, Queen of Salsa	Chambers, Veronica	Dial/2005	9780803729704
We the People: The Story of Our Constitution	Cheney, Lynne	Simon & Schuster/2008	9781416954187
Bodies from the Ice: Melting Glaciers and the Recovery of the Past	Deem, James	Houghton Mifflin/2008	9780618800452

Title	Author (Last, First)	Publisher/Year	ISBN
Washington at Valley Forge	Freedman, Russell	Holiday House/2008	9780823420698
A Tugging String	Greenberg, David	Dutton/2008	9780525479673
Potlatch: A Tsimshian Celebration	Hoyt-Goldsmith, Diane	Holiday House/1997	9780823412907
The Year of the Dog	Lin, Grace	Little, Brown & Company/2006	9780316060028
On the Wings of Heroes	Peck, Richard	Puffin/2007	9780786297030
Escape from Saigon	Warren, Andrea	Farrar, Straus & Giroux/2004	9780374322243
The Day the World Exploded: The Earthshaking Catastrophe at Krakatoa	Winchester, Simon	HarperCollins/2008	9780061239830

Winning Websites

www.readwritethink.org has a lesson entitled "Exploring Cause and Effect Using Expository Texts About Natural Disasters" that promises to help students not only learn about natural disasters but about text structures, too.

www.literacymatters.org/content/study/organizers.htm offers many different graphic organizers that can be used to help guide children through texts.

www.smasd.org/pssa/html/Reading/rihand.htm provides a free handbook that focuses on everything from research on text structure to specific ways to teach it. Specific activities with accompanying examples are included.

Handy Hints

1. Although the selective reading guide was originally created to help students read content-area texts, consider using them to help students read nonfiction children's literature selections as needed.

2. To help students better understand how to determine important information, divide them into groups and assign each group a chapter. Have the group come to an agreement on five important points from the reading. Then, have them use their list to create a selective reading guide for the rest of the class to use when reading their assigned chapter.

3. Sometimes other reading guides are more suited to the reading at hand. Choose another guide from one of the websites listed previously and use it to engage students with their texts. Beyond the websites, another helpful resource is *Guiding Readers Through Text, Second Edition* by Wood, Flood, Lapp, and Taylor (2007).

Poetry Circle

Instructional Information

Poetry is a complex and beautiful genre that is meant to be read aloud. The appreciation of poetry comes from not only from the words on the page but also the performance. Because of poetry's rhythm, repetition, and rhyme, it is a perfect way for ELLs to increase their oral language proficiency and expose them to language (Hadaway, Vardell, and Young 2001). Both academic and communicative language can be used to discuss poems as ELLs move to higher levels of proficiency (Hadaway, Vardell, and Young 2001). The *Poetry Circle* is one way to structure these poetry discussions.

While students at the *bridging* level have strong control over their language use, *Poetry Circle* encourages abstract thinking to accompany students' poetry readings, discussions, and performances in small-group settings. This collaborative learning provides motivation for authentic listening and speaking opportunities, encourages discussion about academic content, and offers a broad spectrum of language from teachers and students (Scarcella and Oxford 1992). Similar to a literature circle, in *Poetry Circle* students come together to discuss, respond, and reflect on their reading. The difference with this activity is that students will add two new components: rehearsal and performance.

Savvy Suggestions

1. Show students your love of poetry by displaying student and professional poetry around the room and on bulletin boards. Create specific tub(s) of books of poetry.

2. After performing a couple of your favorite poems, tell students that they are going to have an opportunity to read, select, discuss, and perform poems that they enjoy from books in the poetry tub.

3. Tell students how *Poetry Circle* (twenty minutes) is organized for the week and post a poetry chart with daily events for their small group of approximately four to six students:

- **Monday:** Browse through poetry texts to select a poem and practice reading the poem to themselves as many times as they possibly can.
- **Tuesday:** Silently read the poem and rehearse with a friend trying on different voices, using different phrases, and reading at different rates.
- **Wednesday, Thursday, Friday:** Poetry Share. Two volunteers per day can perform their poem. Once they have finished the performance, open it up for discussion by asking questions such as, "What is the poem mainly about? What do you think the author was trying to say? How are these poems similar/different?" After discussing the poem's content, allow time for audience members to tell the performer what they liked about the poetry performance.

4. Remind students that the purpose of *Poetry Circle* is to give them some time to explore language and to demonstrate their understanding of poetry.

Classroom Conversations

Sandy is a fourth-grade teacher who wanted to find a way to expose her students to rich and meaningful experiences with text. Her desire led her to consider how she could integrate poetry into her small-group literacy instruction. She decided to use *Poetry Circle* as a means to pique students' interest and introduce poetry not only as a literature genre but also as a performance art. Her *bridging* ELLs are proficient English language users (i.e., reading, writing, speaking, and listening). She believes that poetry and performance will only challenge and enhance their comprehension development. She organizes students into heterogeneous groups of four to six students and allows twenty minutes daily for *Poetry Circle*.

Sandy introduces the new activity by reading aloud two of her favorite poems from *Voice from Afar: Poems of Peace* (Johnston 2008). As Sandy performs the poem, she uses expression, exaggerates the rise and fall of her voice, emphasizes the rate of reading, and gets louder and softer according to the text. The students sit quietly in awe as she finishes her performance and says, "I absolutely love poetry. It is so beautiful when it is performed. You are going to have a chance to select poems that you like to read, rehearse, perform, and discuss too! I have put all the poetry books in these tubs. You get to look through the tubs and find a poem that you would like to perform this week. Here's how our poetry time is going to be organized." She points to the daily chart that shows the *Poetry Circle* events. Sandy gives students time to hover over the book tubs looking for a poetry book they want to use to find a poem they can prepare. Books selected, the students return to their desks and begin their browsing while Sandy walks around talking to students about what they like and what poems they are thinking about selecting. After she see that everyone has selected a poem, she tells them to read it independently a couple of times and start thinking about the different voices, rates, phrases, and volumes they could use in their performance to help convey the meaning.

The following day, Sandy points to the *Poetry Circle* events chart and reminds students of the day's happenings. On Wednesday, the first two performances take place and the students respond with loud applause after Nikki and Tia perform. Sandy asks, "What were the poems mainly about?"

Jack responds, "Well, Nikki's was sad and about being poor, but Tia's was about the new kid on the block."

"After hearing those two poems, what do you think the author was trying to convey?" Sandy questions.

Georgia replies, "I think Nikki's poem was trying to tell us about how hard it is to be poor, how kids go hungry and pray for food. I think the author wants to make the readers aware of what it's like."

The discussion continues as Sandy helps facilitate by asking open-ended questions and allowing students to share their perspectives. The sharing continues on Thursday and Friday. Sandy summarizes the first week by saying, "Poetry is so beautiful, and I love hearing and seeing your fantastic poetry performances. Remember that the performance of your poem is a reflection of your understanding and affects the way the audience perceives and comprehends the poem. We read, rehearse, and perform poetry for enjoyment, and I can't wait to see what you choose to perform next week!"

Terrific Texts for *Poetry Circle*

Title	Author (Last, First)	Publisher/Year	ISBN
School Fever	Bagert, Brod	Dial/2008	9780803732018
Dirt on My Shirt	Foxworthy, Jeff	HarperCollins/2008	9780061208478
Thanks a Million	Grimes, Nikki	Amistad/2006	9780688172930
Voice from Afar: Poems of Peace	Johnston, Tony	Holiday House/2008	9780823420124
The World's Greatest: Poems	Lewis, J. Patrick	Chronicle/2008	9780811851305
Finding Home	Markle, Sandra	Charlesbridge/2008	9781580891226
Awful Ogre Running Wild	Prelutsky, Jack	Greenwillow/2008	9780066238661
The Blacker the Berry	Thomas, Joyce	Joanna Cotler Books/2008	9780060253752
I Don't Want to Clean My Room: A Mess of Poems About Chores	Vestergaard, Hope	Dutton/2007	9780525477761
Barefoot: Poems for Naked Feet	Weisburd, Stefi	Wordsong/2008	9781590783061

Winning Websites

www.ac-nancy-metz.fr/enseign/anglais/Henry/poems.htm
includes a poetry dictionary, types of poetry, poems to read, activities, listening material and lesson plans.

**www.tooter4kids.com/classroom/poetry_in_the_esl_classroom
.htm** is a website specifically designated to using poetry in the ESL
classroom.

http://teachers.net/lessonplans/posts/3073.html has a lesson plan
for using poetry in the ESL elementary classroom.

Handy Hints

1. Instead of allowing students to select their own book and poem
   each week, have students read poems from the same poetry book.
   Students start the week by reading and familiarizing themselves
   with the different poems contained within the book. Then, students select one poem from the text and rehearse for their performance. At the end of the week or during the following week,
   encourage students to share and discuss how their poems relate in
   terms of their content, themes, and similarities and differences.

2. Invite students to bring in bilingual poetry to share with the
   group. Students can provide some background knowledge in English about the poem before performing in their first language.
   The teacher can highlight the influence that different voices,
   phrasing, intonation, and volume can have on conveying meaning
   even when it is performed in an unfamiliar language.

3. After a couple of exposures to *Poetry Circle*, students can create
   their own poetry. After writing a couple of poems, ask students to
   select one to rehearse, perform, and discuss at the end of the week
   if they so choose. Following the performances, make copies of the
   poems that were performed and publish a group poetry book and
   place it in the tubs of poetry books. The group poetry book then
   becomes a resource for other students in years to come when participating in *Poetry Circle*.

Let's Get Critical

Instructional Information

No doubt about it! With the many advertisements, books, and the like bombarding children daily, learning how to read with a critical eye is essential. As I see it, critical reading is comprehending a written message and analyzing it to determine just how true it is. It calls on readers to think about what is read looking for faulty logic or statements with little support, and there is little question that this type of reading demands deep thinking. Readers must be able to evaluate what is being read. In order to make judgments, readers need to be able to collect, interpret, apply, analyze, and synthesize what they are reading. This is just the type of reading that *bridging* ELLs and their classmates are ready to take on. They are adept at using English and are able to engage in lively, thought-provoking discussions.

Let's Get Critical is one way to teach *all* students how to be critical readers. Primarily aimed at helping students recognize bias, teachers scaffold students' learning by first having students listen to and discuss a selection and pointing out how to detect bias. For example, children can listen to determine how a story is told. If they hear "I" a lot, teachers can point out that the story is written in first person and is biased in favor of the storyteller. Students then use the same skill when reading silently.

Savvy Suggestions

1. Select a text that focuses on one person's biased view of the story.

2. Discuss with students what critical listening and reading are and why being a critical listener and reader is important.

3. Prepare students by eliciting their ideas about bias and elaborating on their ideas as needed. Also explain that when they listen or read for one person's perspective, or bias, they are being critical.

4. Tell students that you are going to give them some practice with being critical listeners by reading them a text and seeing if they can determine the bias.

5. Begin reading the text, stopping along the way to ask questions focused on critical listening.

6. Once finished, tell students that critical readers follow the same procedure you just did together when they read.

7. Provide students with time to practice reading and posing questions that show their critical reader stance.

Classroom Conversations

As a result of listening to a group of his third-grade students, Shawn realizes that he needs to teach them how to be more critical in what they are reading. Rather than accepting authors' ideas without question, he wants them to see that readers need to read with the understanding that authors have biases and these show up in the way the text is written. He wants them to develop this understanding so that they will be able to understand the text at hand and make some decisions about whether they want to go along with the author's proposed ideas. Shawn selects *Uncle Peter's Amazing Chinese Wedding* (Look 2006). He opens the lesson by talking with students about critical listening and reading and why knowing how to do both are important. He then tells students to listen to the story to determine the bias. He reads the first page, "This is uncle's brother . . . the coolest dude . . . ," stops and says, "Perfect! Right away I can see that this girl wants me to think that her Uncle Peter is the best person around. She's showing her bias. I don't think I agree with that." Shawn continues reading, inviting students to listen for the storyteller's bias and to comment on what it is she wants them to believe. Once the reading is finished, Shawn comments, "Whether listening or reading, by figuring out the perspective or bias, you can better comprehend what is being said. You can be aware of the bias and decide if you want to agree or disagree with it. Give it a try today during independent reading time. See if you can determine the bias presented in the book and be ready to tell how you know."

Terrific Texts for *Let's Get Critical*

Title	Author (Last, First)	Publisher/Year	ISBN
Up Close: Frank Lloyd Wright: A Twentieth-Century Life	Adkins, Jan	Puffin/2007	9780142412442
The Butter Man	Alalou, Elizabeth Alalou, Ali	Charlesbridge/2008	9781580891271
Timbuktu	Auster, Paul	Minedition/1992	9780698400900
Great Estimations	Goldstone, Bruce	Henry Holt & Company/2008	9780805074468
Uncle Peter's Amazing Chinese Wedding	Look, Lenore	Atheneum/2006	9780689844584
Boycott Blues: How Rosa Parks Inspired a Nation	Pinkney, Andrea	Greenwillow/2008	9780060821180
Wanda Gag: The Girl Who Lived to Draw	Ray, Deborah Kogan	Viking/2008	9780670062928
The Tree	Ruelle, Karen Gray	Holiday House/2008	9780823419043
This Is the Dream	Shore, Diane Alexander, Jessica	Amistad/2006	9780060555207
Underwear: What We Wear Under There	Swain, Ruth Freeman	Holiday House/2008	9780823419203

Winning Websites

www.reading-gamebook.com is filled with ideas designed to boost critical reading and thinking.

www.econedlink.org/lessons/index.cfm?lesson=EM647&page= teacher shows a lesson that affords students with the challenge of helping others make more informed choices when shopping by creating a list of how to detect facts and opinions in advertisements.

www.nationalgeographic.com/xpeditions/lessons/17/g68 /hiddenhistory.html gives students some Native American quotations to interpret.

Handy Hints

1. There are many other skills associated with critical listening/reading including determining fact from opinion. Give students some practice with identifying fact from opinion by bringing in newspaper articles or other interesting material and reading them to students. Have students identify facts and opinions and provide reasons for their answers.

2. Being able to recognize emotive words is yet another critical listening/reading skill. After providing students with some examples (e.g., *amazing, incredible, beautiful*) and showing them that emotion is often carried by the manner in which the words are stated, have them find their own examples of statements that have emotive words and read them to others trying to evoke the intended emotion.

Children's Literature

Adkins, J. 2007. *Up Close: Frank Lloyd Wright: A Twentieth-Century Life*. New York: Puffin.

Adler, D. A. 2006. *You Can, Toucan, Math: Word Problem-Solving Fun*. New York: Holiday House.

Ajmera, M., and J. D. Ivanko. 1999. *To Be a Kid*. Watertown, MA: Charlesbridge.

Alalou, E., and A. Alalou. 2008. *The Butter Man*. Watertown, MA: Charlesbridge.

Andreae, G. 2007. *Captain Flinn and the Pirate Dinosaurs: Missing Treasure!* New York: Margaret K. McElderry Books.

Arnosky, J. 2007. *Babies in the Bayou*. New York: G.P. Putnam's Sons.

Aston, D. 2008. *Not So Tall for Six*. Watertown, MA: Charlesbridge.

Aston, D. H. 2008. *The Moon over Star*. New York: Dial Books for Young Readers.

Auch, M. J. 2007. *Beauty and the Beaks: A Turkey's Cautionary Tale*. New York: Holiday House.

Auster, P. 1992. *Timbuktu*. New York: Minedition.

Ayres, K. 2007. *Up, Down, and Around*. Cambridge, MA: Candlewick.

Bagert, B. 2008. *School Fever*. New York: Dial Books for Young Readers.

Baker, K. 2007. *Hickory Dickory Dock*. New York: Harcourt.

Barretta, G. 2006. *Now & Ben: The Modern Inventions of Benjamin Franklin*. New York: Henry Holt & Company.

Beaumont, K. 2008. *Doggone Dogs*. New York: Dial Books for Young Readers.

Bee, W. 2008. *Beware of the Frog*. Cambridge, MA: Candlewick.

Beil, K. M. 2008. *Jack's House*. New York: Holiday House.

Berger, C. 2008. *The Little Yellow Leaf*. New York: Greenwillow.

Bildner, P. 2008. *Turkey Bowl*. New York: Simon & Schuster.

Breathed, B. 2008. *Pete & Pickles*. New York: Philomel.

Breen, S. 2007. *Stick*. New York: Dial Books for Young Readers.

Brennan-Nelson, D. 2004. *My Teacher Likes to Say*. Chelsea, MI: Sleeping Bear Press.

Brett, J. 2008. *Gingerbread Friends*. New York: G.P. Putnam's Sons.

Bridges, S. Y. 2008. *The Umbrella Queen*. New York: Greenwillow.

Brown, C. 2008. *Soup for Breakfast*. Boston: Houghton Mifflin.

Brown, M. W. 2007. *Goodnight Moon 123/Buenas noches, luna 123*. New York: Rayo.

Buehner, C., and M. Buehner. 2008. *The Queen of Style*. New York: Dial Books for Young Readers.

Bunting, E. 2007. *Hurry! Hurry!* Orlando: Harcourt.

———. 2008. *Walking to School*. New York: Clarion.

Carter, D. 2006. *Woof! Woof!* New York: Little Simon.

Chambers, V. 2005. *Celia Cruz, Queen of Salsa*. New York: Dial Books for Young Readers.

Cheney, L. 2008. *We the People: The Story of Our Constitution*. New York: Simon & Schuster.

Chessa, F. 2008. *Holly's Red Boots*. New York: Holiday House.

Chocolate, D. 2009. *El Barrio*. New York: Holt.

Church, C. J. 2008. *Ping Pong Pig*. New York: Holiday House.

Cohan, G. 2008. *Norman Rockwell: You're a Grand Old Flag*. New York: Atheneum Books for Young Readers.

Collard, S. B. 2008. *Teeth*. Watertown, MA: Charlesbridge.

Cordsen, C. F. 2008. *Market Day*. New York: Dutton Children's Books.

Covert, R. 2008. *Ralph's World Rocks!* New York: Henry Holt & Company.

Cronin, D. 2008. *Thump, Quack, Moo: A Whacky Adventure*. New York: Atheneum.

Crow, K. 2008. *Bedtime at the Swamp*. New York: HarperCollins.

Cruise, R. 2006. *Little Mama Forgets*. New York: Melanie Kroupa Books.

Cunnane, K. 2006. *For You Are a Kenyan Child*. New York: Atheneum Books for Young Readers.

Curtis, J. L. 2008. *Big Words for Little People*. New York: HarperCollins.

Davis, N. 2003. *Surprising Sharks*. Cambridge, MA: Candlewick.

Day, A. 2008. *Carl's Summer Vacation*. New York: Farrar, Straus & Giroux.

De La Hoya, O., and M. Shulman. 2006. *Super Oscar*. New York: Simon & Schuster Books for Young Readers.

Deem, J. M. 2008. *Bodies from the Ice: Melting Glaciers and the Recovery of the Past*. Boston: Houghton Mifflin.

Demi. 2008. *The Girl Who Drew a Phoenix*. New York: Margaret K. McElderry Books.

Diakite, P. 2006. *I Lost My Tooth in Africa*. New York: Scholastic.

Diesen, D. 2008. *The Pout-Pout Fish*. New York: Farrar, Straus & Giroux.

Dillon, L., and D. Dillion. 2007. *Mother Goose Numbers on the Loose*. Orlando: Harcourt.

DK Publishing. 2006. *Signs in Our World*. New York: DK Children.

Donaldson, J. 2007. *The Fish Who Cried Wolf*. New York: Arthur A. Levine Books.

———. 2008. *Where's My Mom?* New York: Dial Books for Young Readers.

Dooling, M. 2005. *Young Thomas Edison*. New York: Holiday House.

Dorros, A. 2008. *Papa and Me*. New York: Rayo.

Downing, J. 2008. *No Hugs Till Saturday*. New York: Clarion.

Doyle, M. 2008. *Horse*. New York: Margaret K. McElderry Books.

Dylan, B. 2008. *Forever Young*. New York: Ginee Seo Books.

Edwards, P. D. 2008. *Jack and Jill's Treehouse*. New York: Katherine Tegen Books.

Elliott, D. 2008. *Wuv Bunnies from Outers Pace*. New York: Holiday House.

Elya, S. M. 2003. *Oh No, Gotta Go!* New York: G.P. Putnam's Sons.

———. 2006. *Bebe Goes Shopping*. Orlando: Harcourt.

———. 2006. *F Is for Fiesta*. New York: G.P. Putnam's Sons.

———. 2008. *Tooth on the Loose*. New York: G.P. Putnam's Sons.

Emmett, J. 2006. *She'll Be Coming 'Round the Mountain*. New York: Simon & Schuster.

Engelbreit, M. 2008. *Mary Engelbreit's Mother Goose Favorites*. New York: HarperCollins.

Faller, R. 2007. *Polo: The Runaway Book*. New York: Roaring Brook Press.

Fenton, J. 2008. *What's Under the Bed?* New York: Simon & Schuster.

Fleming, D. 2007. *Beetle Bop*. Orlando: Harcourt.

Florian, D. 2003. *Bow Wow Meow Meow: It's Rhyming Cats and Dogs*. San Diego: Harcourt.

Foley, G. 2008. *Don't Worry Bear*. New York: Viking.

Foreman, J. 2008. *Say Hello*. Cambridge, MA: Candlewick.

Foxworthy, J. 2008. *Dirt on My Shirt*. New York: HarperCollins.

Franco, B. 2008. *Bees, Snails, and Peacock Tails*. New York: Margaret K. McElderry Books.

Freedman, R. 2008. *Washington at Valley Forge*. New York: Holiday House.

Freeman, D. 2008. *Corduroy (40th anniversary edition)*. New York: Viking.

Garland, M. 2006. *Miss Smith Reads Again!* New York: Dutton Children's Books.

———. 2008. *Americana Adventure*. New York: Dutton Children's Books.

George, J. C. 2008. *The Wolves Are Back*. New York: Dutton Children's Books.

George, L. B. 2008. *Alfred Digs*. New York: Greenwillow.

Gibbons, G. 2008. *Dinosaurs!* New York: Holiday House.

———. 2008. *Elephants of Africa*. New York: Holiday House.

Giovanni, N. 2008. *Lincoln and Douglass: An American Friendship*. New York: Henry Holt & Company.

Goldfinger, J. P. 2007. *My Dog Lyle*. New York: Clarion.

Goldstone, B. 2008. *Great Estimations*. New York: Henry Holt & Company.

Graham, T. 2008. *Five Little Firefighters*. New York: Henry Holt & Company.

Gray, R. 2008. *Mama Mine, Mama Mine*. New York: Dutton Children's Books.

Greenberg, D. T. 2008. *A Tugging String*. New York: Dutton Children's Books.

Grimes, N. 2006. *Oh, Brother!* New York: Greenwillow.

———. 2006. *Thanks a Million*. New York: Amistad/HarperCollins.

Hague, M. 2008. *The Book of Wizards*. New York: HarperCollins.

Hale, B. 2008. *Flyboy of Underwhere*. New York: HarperCollins.

———. 2008. *Pirates of Underwhere*. New York: HarperCollins.

Harby, M. 2007. *All Aboard for Dreamland!* New York: Simon & Schuster Books for Young Readers.

Heling, K., and D. Hembrook. 2008. *Midnight Fright*. New York: Scholastic.

Henkes, K. 2008. *Bird Lake Moon*. New York: Greenwillow.

———. 2008. *Old Bear*. New York: Greenwillow.

Henson, H. 2008. *That Book Woman*. New York: Atheneum.

Hill, M. 2003. *Signs at School*. New York: Children's Press.

———. 2003. *Signs at the Park*. New York: Children's Press.

———. 2003. *Signs at the Store*. New York: Children's Press.

Hoban, T. 1983. *I Read Symbols!* New York: Greenwillow.

———. 1987. *I Read Signs!* New York: HarperTrophy.

———. 1995. *Colors Everywhere.* New York: Greenwillow.

Hobbs, W. 2008. *Go Big or Go Home.* New York: HarperCollins.

Hopkins, L. B. 2004. *Wonderful Words.* New York: Simon & Schuster.

Horacek, P. 2007. *Butterfly, Butterfly.* Cambridge, MA: Candlewick.

Horowitz, D. 2008. *Humpty Dumpty Climbs Again.* New York: G.P. Putnam's Sons.

———. 2008. *Twenty-Six Princesses.* New York: G.P. Putnam's Sons.

Howe, P. 2008. *Waggit's Tale.* New York: HarperCollins.

Howland, N. 1994. *ABC Drive!* New York: Clarion.

Hoyt-Goldsmith, D. 1997. *Potlatch: A Tsimshian Celebration.* New York: Holiday House.

Hunter, E. 2008. *Power of Three Warriors Outcast.* New York: HarperCollins.

———. 2008. *Power of Three Warriors: Dark River.* New York: HarperCollins.

———. 2008. *Seekers: The Quest Begins.* New York: HarperCollins.

Ichikawa, S. 2008. *Come Fly with Me.* New York: Philomel.

Isadora, R. 2006. *What a Family!* New York: G.P. Putnam's Sons.

Jackson, E. 2008. *A Home for Dixie.* New York: HarperCollins.

Jeffers, O. 2007. *The Way Back Home.* New York: Philomel.

Jenkins, S., and R. Page. 2008. *How Many Ways Can You Catch a Fly?* Boston: Houghton Mifflin.

Jimenez, F. 2008. *Reaching Out.* Boston: Houghton Mifflin.

Johnson, A. 2007. *Wind Flyers.* New York: Simon & Schuster.

Johnson, S. T. 2008. *A Is for Art: An Abstract Alphabet.* New York: Paula Wiseman Books/Simon & Schuster.

Johnston, T. 2008. *Voice from Afar: Poems of Peace.* New York: Holiday House.

Joosse, B. 2008. *Grandma Calls Me Beautiful.* San Francisco: Chronicle.

———. 2008. *In the Night Garden.* New York: Henry Holt & Company.

Katz, K. 2006. *Can You Say Peace?* New York: Henry Holt & Company.

Keats, E. J., and J. N. Harrington. 2008. *Roberto Walks Home.* New York: Viking.

Khan, H. 2008. *Night of the Moon.* San Francisco: Chronicle.

Kimmel, E. A. 2008. *Stormy's Hat: Just Right for a Railroad Man*. New York: Farrar, Straus & Giroux.

Kleven, E. 2005. *The Paper Princess Flies Again: With Her Dog!* Berkeley, CA: Tricycle.

Kolar, B. 2003. *Racer Dogs*. New York: Dutton Children's Books.

Koller, J. F. 2008. *Peter Spit a Seed at Sue*. New York: Viking.

Krensky, S. 2008. *A Man for All Seasons: The Life of George Washington Carver*. New York: Amistad.

———. 2008. *Spark the Firefighter*. New York: Dutton Children's Books.

Kruusval, C. 2008. *Ellen's Apple Tree*. New York: R & S Books.

Kudlinski, K. V. 2005. *Boy, Were We Wrong About Dinosaurs!* New York: Puffin.

Kvasnosky, L. M. 2008. *Really Truly Bingo*. Cambridge, MA: Candlewick.

Lakin, P. 2007. *Rainy Day!* New York: Dial Books for Young Readers.

Langton, J. 2008. *The Dragon Tree*. New York: HarperCollins.

Lanthier, J. 2006. *The Mystery of the Martello Tower*. New York: Laura Geringer Books.

Lasky, K. 2003. *A Voice of Her Own: The Story of Phillis Weatley, Slave Poet*. Cambridge, MA: Candlewick.

———. 2006. *John Muir: America's First Environmentalist*. Cambridge, MA: Candlewick.

Lee, S. 2008. *Wave*. San Francisco: Chronicle.

Leedy, L. 2008. *Crazy Like a Fox: A Simile Story*. New York: Holiday House.

Leeper, A. 2004. *Grocery Store*. Chicago: Heinemann Raintree.

Lehman, B. 2008. *Trainstop*. Boston: Houghton Mifflin.

Lewin, T. 2006. *How Much? Visiting Markets Around the World*. New York: HarperCollins.

Lewis, J. P. 2008. *The World's Greatest: Poems*. San Francisco: Chronicle.

LeZotte, A. C. 2008. *T4*. New York: Houghton Mifflin.

Lies, B. 2008. *Bats at the Library*. Boston: Houghton Mifflin.

Lin, G. 2006. *The Year of the Dog*. New York: Little, Brown & Company.

Lithgow, J. 2008. *I Got Two Dogs*. New York: Simon & Schuster.

Livingston, I. 2003. *Finklehopper Frog*. Berkeley, CA: Tricycle.

Liwska, R. 2008. *Little Panda*. Boston: Houghton Mifflin.

Ljungkvist, L. 2008. *Follow the Line Around the World*. New York: Viking.

Look, L. 2006. *Uncle Peter's Amazing Chinese Wedding*. New York: Atheneum Books for Young Readers.

Lucas, D. 2007. *The Robot and the Bluebird*. New York: Farrar, Straus & Giroux.

Lyon, G. E. 2008. *My Friend, the Starfinder*. New York: Antheneum Books for Young Readers.

Macken, J. E. 2008. *Flip, Float, Fly Seeds on the Move*. New York: Holiday House.

Manning, J. 2008. *Cat Nights*. New York: Greenwillow.

Manning, M. J. 2008. *Kitchen Dance*. New York: Clarion.

Markle, S. 2008. *Finding Home*. Watertown, MA: Charlesbridge.

Martin, B. 1970. *Brown Bear, Brown Bear, What Do You See?* New York: Holt.

Martino, C. A. 2005. *Rosa, Sola*. Cambridge, MA: Candlewick.

McDonald, M. 2008. *Hen Hears Gossip*. New York: Greenwillow.

McMillan, B., and J. A. Music. 2008. *Sharks*. New York: Simon & Schuster Books for Young Readers.

Melmed, L. K. 2008. *Hurry! Hurry! Have You Heard?* San Francisco: Chronicle.

Meserve, J. 2008. *Can Anybody Hear Me?* New York: Clarion.

Metzger, S. 2005. *We're Going on a Leaf Hunt*. New York: Scholastic.

Milich, Z. 2008. *City Signs*. Toronto, ON: Kids Can Press.

Milusich, J. 2008. *Off Go Their Engines, Off Go Their Lights*. New York: Dutton Children's Books.

Mora, P. 2008. *Here, Kitty, Kitty!/Ven, Gatita, ven!* New York: Rayo.

———. 2009. *Book Fiesta! Celebrate Children's Day/Book Day/Celebremos El dia de los ninos/El dia de los libros*. New York: HarperCollins.

Moses, W. 2008. *Raining Cats and Dogs*. New York: Philomel.

Moustaki, N. 2008. *Dogfessions: Secret Confessions from Dogs*. New York: HarperCollins.

Nedwidek, J. 2008. *Ducks Don't Wear Socks*. New York: Viking.

Nikola-Lisa, W. 1997. *America: My Land, Your Land, Our Land*. New York: Lee & Low.

Nodset, J. L. 2008. *Come Back, Cat*. New York: HarperCollins.

Nyeu, T. 2008. *Wonder Bear*. New York: Dial Books for Young Readers.

O'Conner, J. 2008. *Fancy Nancy's Favorite Fancy Words from Accessories to Zany*. New York: HarperCollins.

Parish, H. 2008. *Amelia Bedelia Talks Turkey*. New York: Greenwillow.

Paver, M. 2008. *Outcast*. New York: HarperCollins.

Peck, R. 2007. *On the Wings of Heroes*. New York: Puffin.

Pedersen, J. 2008. *Houdini the Amazing Caterpillar*. New York: Clarion.

Pelletier, D. 1999. *Alphabet City*. New York: Puffin.

Perkins, L. R. 2008. *The Cardboard Piano*. New York: Greenwillow.

Perry, A. 2007. *The Snack Smasher and Other Reasons Why It's Not My Fault*. New York: Atheneum Books for Young Readers.

Pinkney, A. D. 2008. *Boycott Blues: How Rosa Parks Inspired a Nation*. New York: Greenwillow.

Pinkney, B. 2006. *Hush, Little Baby*. New York: Greenwillow.

Plourde, L. 2001. *Winter Waits*. New York: Simon & Schuster Books for Young Readers.

Polacco, P. 2005. *Emma Kate*. New York: Puffin.

———. 2008. *For the Love of Autumn*. New York: Philomel.

Poydar, N. 2008. *Zip, Zip . . . Homework*. New York: Holiday House.

Prelutsky, J. 2008. *Awful Ogre Running Wild*. New York: Greenwillow.

Rabin, S. 2008. *Mr. Lincoln's Boys*. New York: Viking.

Ramos, J. 2008. *I'm Just Like My Mom/I'm Just Like My Dad: Me parezco tanto a mi mama/Me parezco tanto a mi papa*. New York: HarperCollins.

Raschka, C. 2008. *Peter and the Wolf*. New York: Atheneum.

Raskin, E. 1978. *The Westing Game*. New York: Penguin.

Ray, D. K. 2008. *Wanda Gag: The Girl Who Lived to Draw*. New York: Viking.

Reiser, L. 1998. *Tortillas and Lullabies, Tortillas y cancioncitas*. New York: Greenwillow.

Rex, M. 2008. *Goodnight Goon: A Petrifying Parody*. New York: G.P. Putnam's Sons.

Ries, L. 2008. *Punk Wig*. Honesdale, PA: Boyds Mills Press.

Roehrig, C. 2008. *Fun with Hieroglyphs*. New York: Metropolitan Museum of Art/Simon & Schuster.

Rosen, M., and H. Oxenbury. 2007. *We're Going on a Bear Hunt*. New York: Little Simon.

Rosenthal, A. K. 2008. *It's Not Fair!* New York: HarperCollins.

———. 2008. *Little Hoot*. San Francisco: Chronicle.

Rowe, J. A. 2008. *Smile*. New York: Penguin Young Readers Group.

Ruelle, K.G. 2008. *The Tree*. New York: Holiday House.

Rumford, J. 2008. *Chee-Lin: A Giraffe's Journey*. Boston: Houghton Mifflin.

Rylant, C. 1998. *Scarecrow*. San Diego: Harcourt Brace & Company.

Sayre, A. P. 2008. *Trout Are Made of Trees*. Watertown, MA: Charlesbridge.

Schachner, J. 2006. *Skippyjon Jones in Mummy Trouble*. New York: Puffin.

Schaefer, C. 2008. *Kids Like Us*. New York: Viking.

Schoenherr, I. 2008. *Cat & Mouse*. New York: Greenwillow.

Schotter, R. 2008. *The House of Joyful Living*. New York: Melanie Kroupa Books.

Schubert, I., and D. Schubert. 2008. *Like People*. Asheville, NC: Lemniscaat.

Scieszka, J. 2008. *Melvin Might?* New York: Simon & Schuster.

Scott, E. 2008. *All About Sleep from A to Zzzz*. New York: Viking.

Scotton, R. 2008. *Splat the Cat*. New York: HarperCollins.

Seibold, J. O., and S. Vivian. 2008. *Vunce Upon a Time*. San Francisco: Chronicle.

Seskin, S., and A. Shamblin. 2002. *Don't Laugh at Me*. Berkeley, CA: Tricycle.

Shapiro, J. F. 2003. *Up, Up, Up! It's Apple-Picking Time*. New York: Holiday House.

Sherry, K. 2008. *I'm the Best Artist in the Ocean*. New York: Dial Books for Young Readers.

Shore, D. Z. 2008. *This Is the Feast*. New York: HarperCollins.

Shore, D. Z., and J. Alexander. 2006. *This Is the Dream*. New York: Amistad.

Silverman, E. 2008. *There Was a Wee Woman*. New York: Melanie Kroupa Books.

Snow, M. 2008. *Sisters of the Sword*. New York: HarperCollins.

Spinelli, J. 2008. *Smiles to Go*. New York: Joanna Cotler Books.

Stadler, A. 2003. *Beverly Billingsly Takes a Bow*. San Diego: Harcourt.

Stainton, S. 2007. *I Love Cats*. New York: Katherine Tegen Books.

Stein, D. E. 2008. *The Nice Book*. New York: G.P. Putnam's Sons.

Stiegemeyer, J. 2008. *Gobble Gobble Crash! A Barnyard Counting Bash*. New York: Dutton Children's Books.

Stojic, M. 2002. *Hello World! Greetings in 42 Languages Around the Globe!* New York: Cartwheel.

Stone, T. L. 2008. *Sandy's Circus: A Story About Alexander Calder*. New York: Viking.

Sutton, S. 2008. *Roadwork*. Cambridge, MA: Candlewick.

Swain, R. F. 2008. *Underwear: What We Wear Under There*. New York: Holiday House.

Tabor, N. 2000. *Ve lo que dices: Modismos en español e inglés (See What You Say: Spanish and English Idioms)*. Watertown, MA: Charlesbridge.

Tafuri, N. 2008. *Blue Goose*. New York: Simon & Schuster Books for Young Readers.

Tait, N. 2008. *Insects & Spiders*. New York: Simon & Schuster Books for Young Readers.

Tankard, J. 2008. *Me Hungry!* Cambridge, MA: Candlewick.

Terban, M. 2008. *The Dove Dove: Funny Homograph Riddles*. New York: Clarion.

Thomas, J. C. 2008. *The Blacker the Berry*. New York: Joanna Cotler.

Thomson, S. L. 2008. *Imagine a Place*. New York: Atheneum.

Vail, R. 2008. *Lucky*. New York: HarperCollins.

Vestergaard, H. 2007. *I Don't Want to Clean My Room: A Mess of Poems About Chores*. New York: Dutton Children's Books.

Vila, L. 2008. *Building Manhattan*. New York: Viking.

Viorst, J. 2008. *Nobody Here But Me*. New York: Farrar, Straus & Giroux.

Warnes, T. 2008. *Chalk & Cheese*. New York: Simon & Schuster.

Warren, A. 2004. *Escape from Saigon*. New York: Farrar, Straus & Giroux.

Weaver, T. 2008. *Frederick Finch, Loudmouth*. New York: Clarion.

Weisburd, S. 2008. *Barefoot: Poems for Naked Feet*. Honesdale, PA: Wordsong.

Wells, R. 2008. *Otto Runs for President*. New York: Scholastic.

Whitehead, K., and S. W. Evans. 2008. *Art from Her Heart: Folk Artist*. New York: G.P. Putnam's Sons.

Wickberg, S. 2008. *Hey Mr. Choo-choo, Where Are You Going?* New York: G.P. Putnam's Sons.

Wiesner, D. 2006. *Flotsam*. New York: Clarion.

Wilhelm, H. 2008. *Come Rhyme with Me!* New York: Scholastic.

Willey, M. 2008. *The 3 Bears and Goldilocks*. New York: Atheneum.

Williams, A. 2005. *Tiny Tortilla*. New York: Dutton Children's Books.

Williams, C. A. 2008. *Booming Bella*. New York: G.P. Putnam's Sons.

Wilson, K. 2008. *Where Is Home, Little Pip?* New York: Margaret K. McElderry Books.

Winchester, S. 2008. *The Day the World Exploded: The Earthshaking Catastrophe at Krakatoa*. New York: HarperCollins.

Wolf, S. 2008. *Truck Stuck*. Watertown, MA: Charlesbridge.

Yolen, J. 2005. *Meow: Cat Stories from Around the World*. New York: HarperCollins.

Yonezu, Y. 2008. *A Cup for Everyone*. New York: Penguin.

Yoo, T.-E. 2007. *The Little Red Fish*. New York: Penguin/Dial.

Young, E. 2006. *My Mei Mei*. New York: Philomel.

References

Allington, R. 1984. "Oral Reading." In *The Handbook of Reading Research* 1, ed. R. Barr, M. Kamil, and P. Mosenthal, 829–64. New York: Longman.

———. 2006. *What Really Matters for Struggling Readers: Designing Research-Based Programs*. 2d ed. New York: Allyn & Bacon.

Ayers, L. 1993. "The Efficacy of Three Training Conditions on Phonological Awareness of Kindergarten Children and the Longitudinal Effect of Each on Later Reading Acquisition." Ph.D. Dissertation, Oakland University: Rochester, Michigan.

Bauman, J., L. A. Jones, and N. Seifert-Kessell. 1993. "Using Think-Alouds to Increase Children's Comprehension Monitoring Abilities." *The Reading Teacher* 47: 184–89.

Baynham, M. 1993. "Literacy in TESOL and ABE: Exploring Common Themes." *Open Letter* 2: 4–16.

Bizzell, P., and B. Herzberg. 2001. *The Rhetorical Tradition Readings from Classical Times to the Present,* 2d ed. Boston: Bedford/St. Martin's.

Black, A., and A. M. Stave. 2007. *A Comprehensive Guide to Readers' Theater: Enhancing Fluency and Comprehension in Middle School and Beyond.* Newark, NJ: International Reading Association.

Block, C. 1997. *Literacy Difficulties: Diagnosis and Instruction.* San Diego: Harcourt Brace.

Block, C., and S. E. Israel. 2004. "The ABCs of Performing Highly Effective Think-Alouds." *The Reading Teacher* 58: 154–67.

Boyd-Batstone, P. 2006. *Differentiated Early Literacy for English Language Learners*. Boston: Pearson.

Boyle, O. F., and S. F. Peregoy. 1990. "Literacy Scaffolds: Strategies for First- and Second-Language Readers and Writers." *The Reading Teacher* 44: 194–200.

Bradley, J. M., and M. R. Thalgott. 1987. "Reducing Reading Anxiety." *Academic Therapy* 22: 349–58.

Bruner, J. 1978. "The Role of Dialogue in Language Acquisition." In *The Child's Conception of Language*, ed. A. Sinclair, R. Jarvella, and W. Levelt, 204–18. New York: Springer-Verlag.

Cappellini, M. 2005. *Reading & Language Learning: A Resource for Teaching English Language Learners*. Newark, DE: International Reading Association.

Cazden, C. B. 2001. *Classroom Discourse: The Language of Teaching and Learning.* 2d ed. Portsmouth, NH: Heinemann.

Chamot, A., and J. O'Malley. 1994. *The CALLA Handbook: Implementing the Cognitive Academic Language Learning Approach.* Reading, MA: Addison-Wesley.

Chen, L., and E. Mora-Flores. 2006. *Balanced Literacy for English Language Learners, K–2.* Portsmouth, NH: Heinemann.

Chomsky, C. 1976. "After Decoding: What?" *Language Arts* 53: 288–96.

Chomsky, N. 1965. *Aspects of the Theory of Syntax.* Cambridge: M.I.T. Press.

Clay, M. 1979. *The Early Detection of Reading Difficulties.* Portsmouth, NH: Heinemann.

Cohen, D. 1968. "The Effect of Language on Vocabulary and Reading Achievement." *Elementary English* 45: 217.

Cummins, J. 1979. "Linguistic Interdependence and the Educational Development of Bilingual Children." *Review of Educational Research* 49: 221–51.

Cunningham, D., and S. L. Shablak. 1975. "Selective Reading Guide-o-Rama: The Content Teacher's Best Friend." *Journal of Reading* 18: 380–82.

Cunningham, P. M., D. P. Hall, and C. M. Sigmon. 1999. *The Teacher's Guide to the Four Blocks: A Multimethod, Multilevel Framework for Grades 1–3.* Greenville, NC: Carson, Dellosa.

Davey, B. 1983. "Think Aloud—Modeling the Cognitive Processes of Reading Comprehension." *Journal of Reading* 27: 44–47.

DeHaven, E. 1989. *Teaching and Learning the Language Arts.* 3d ed. New York: Scott Foresman.

Diamond, B., and M. Moore. 1995. *Multicultural Literacy: Mirroring the Reality of the Classroom.* White Plains, NY: Longman.

Diaz-Rico, L. T. 2008. *Strategies for Teaching English Learners.* 2d ed. Boston: Pearson.

Diaz-Rico, L. T., and K. Z. Weed. 2002. *The Crosscultural, Language and Academic Development Handbook: A Complete K–12 Reference Guide.* Boston: Allyn & Bacon.

Dickinson, D. K., and M. W. Smith. 1994. "Long-Term Effects of Preschool Teachers' Book Readings on Low-Income Children's Vocabulary and Story Comprehension." *Reading Research Quarterly* 29: 105–22.

Duke, N. K., and P. D. Pearson. 2002. "Effective Practices for Developing Reading Comprehension." In *What Research Has to Say About Reading Instruction*, 3d ed., ed. A. Farstrup and S.J. Samuels, 205–42. Newark, DE: International Reading Association.

Early, M. 1991. "Using Wordless Picture Books to Promote Second Language Learning." *ELT Journal* 45: 245–51.

Edwards, P. 1975. "The Effect of Idioms on Children's Reading and Understanding of Prose." In *Teacher, Tangibles and Techniques: Comprehension of Content in Reading,* ed. B. S. Schulwitz, 37–46. Newark, DE: International Reading Association.

Elley, W. 1989. "Vocabulary Acquisition from Listening to Stories." *Reading Research Quarterly* 24: 174–87.

———. 1991. "Acquiring Literacy in a Second Language: The Effect of Book-Based Programs." *Language Learning* 41: 375–411.

Elley, W., and F. Mangubhai. 1983. "The Impact of Reading on Second Language Learning." *Reading Research Quarterly* 19: 53–67.

Fitzgerald, J. 1993. "Literacy and Students Who Are Learning English as a Second Language." *The Reading Teacher* 46: 638–47.

Flurkey, A. 2006. "What's 'Normal' About Real Reading?" In *The Truth About DIBELS: What It Is and What It Does,* ed. K. Goodman, 40–49. Portsmouth, NH: Heinemann.

Freeman, D. E., and Y. S. Freeman. 2000. *Teaching Reading in Multilingual Classrooms.* Portsmouth, NH: Heinemann.

———. 2007. *English Language Learners: The Essential Guide.* New York: Scholastic.

Gardner, R. C., and W. E. Lambert. 1972. *Attitudes and Motivation in Second Language Learning.* Rowley, MA: Newbury House.

Goodman, K. 1969. *Analysis of Oral Reading Miscues: Applied Psycholinguistics.* Newark, DE: International Reading Association.

Guthrie, J. T., and A. Taboado. 2004. "Fostering the Cognitive Strategies of Reading Comprehension." In *Motivating Reading Comprehension: Concept-Oriented Reading Instruction,* ed. J. T. Guthrie, A. Wigfield, and K. Perencevich, 87–112. Mahwah, NJ: Erlbaum.

Hadaway, N. L., S. M. Vardell, and T. A. Young. 2001. "Scaffolding Oral Language Development Through Poetry for Students Learning English." *The Reading Teacher* 54: 796–806.

———. 2002. *Literature-Based Instruction with English Language Learners, K–12.* Boston: Allyn & Bacon.

Halliday, M. 1975. *Explorations in the Functions of Language.* London: Arnold.

Harris, T., and R. Hodges, eds. 1995. *The Literacy Dictionary.* Newark, DE: International Reading Association.

Harste, J., C. Burke, and V. Woodward. 1982. "Children's Language and World: Initial Encounters with Print." In *Reader Meets Author: Bridging the Gap: A Psycholinguistic and Sociolinguistic Perspective*, ed. J. A. Langer and M. T. Smith-Burke, 105–31. Newark, DE: International Reading Association.

Harste, J. C., K. G. Short, and C. Burke. 1988. *Creating Classrooms for Authors*. Portsmouth, NH: Heinemann.

Hernandez, H. 1989. *Multicultural Education: A Teacher's Guide to Content and Process*. London: Merrill.

Herrell, A. L., and M. Jordan. 2008. *50 Strategies for Teaching English Language Learners*. 3d ed. Upper Saddle River, NJ: Pearson.

Holdaway, D. 1979. *The Foundations of Literacy*. New York: Ashton-Scholastic.

Institute of Educational Sciences. 2008. *Reading First Impact Study: Final Report*. U.S. Department of Education. BCEE 2009-4039.

Irwin, J. W. 1991. *Teaching Reading Comprehension Processes*. 2d ed. Englewood Cliffs, NJ: Prentice Hall.

Jímenez, R. T., G. E. Garcia, and P. D. Pearson. 1996. "The Reading Strategies of Bilingual Latina/o Students Who Are Successful English Readers: Opportunities and Obstacles." *Reading Research Quarterly* 31: 90–112.

Kendal, J., and O. Khuon. 2005. *Making Sense: Small-Group Comprehension Lessons for English Language Learners*. Portland, ME: Stenhouse.

Kennedy, T. 2001. "Classroom Practices for Literacy Development of English Language Learners." *Northwest Passage* (Spring): 35–39.

Krashen, S. 1982. *Principles and Practices in Second Language Acquisition*. Oxford: Pergamon Press.

———. 1983. "Some Working Ideas for Language Teaching." In *Methods That Work: A Smorgasbord of Ideas for Language Teachers,* ed. J. W. Oller and P. A. Richard-Amato, 3–19. New York: Newbury House.

———. 2004. *The Power of Reading: Insights from the Research*. 2d ed. Portsmouth, NH: Heinemann.

Krashen, S., and T. Terrell. 1983. *The Natural Approach: Language Acquisition in the Classroom*. Oxford: Pergamon.

Kuby, P. 1999. "A Review of Research on Environmental Print." *Journal of Instructional Psychology* (Sept.): 1–10.

———. 2004. "The Impact of Environmental Print Instruction on Early Reading Ability." *Journal of Instructional Psychology* (June): 1–8.

Kucer, S. 2005. *Dimensions of Literacy*. 2d ed. Mahwah, NJ: Erlbaum.

Lavadenz, M. 2003. "Think-Aloud Protocols: Teaching Reading Processes to Young Bilingual Students." *ERIC Digest* (EDO-FL-03-14).

Lesaux, N., and E. Geva. 2006. "Synthesis: Development of Literacy in Language-Minority Students." In *Developing Literacy in Second-Language Learners*, ed. D. August and T. Shanahan, 53–74. Mahwah, NJ: Erlbaum.

Li, D., and S. L. Nes. 2001. "Using Paired Reading to Help ESL Students Become Fluent and Accurate Readers." *Reading Improvement* 38: 50–61.

May, A. B. 1979. "All the Angles of Idiom Instruction." *Reading Teacher* 32: 680–82.

McCauley, J., and D. McCauley. 1992. "Using Choral Reading to Promote Language Learning for ESL Students." *The Reading Teacher* 45: 526–33.

McKeown, R. G., and J. Gentilucci. 2007. "Think-Aloud Strategy: Metacognitive Development and Monitoring Comprehension in the Middle School Second-Language Classroom." *Journal of Adult and Adolescent Literacy* 51: 136–47.

Medina, S. 2002. "Using Music to Enhance Second Language Acquisition: From Theory to Practice." In *Language, Literacy and Academic Development for English Language Learners*, ed. J. Lalas and S. Lee. Boston: Pearson.

Mehan, H. 1979. *Learning Lessons: Social Organization in the Classroom*. Cambridge: Harvard University Press.

Meyers, M. 1993. *Teaching to Diversity: Teaching and Learning in the Multiethnic Classroom*. Reading, MA: Addison Wesley.

Miccinati, J. L. 1985. "Using Prosodic Cues to Teach Oral Reading Fluency." *The Reading Teacher* 39: 206–12.

Nickerson, L. 1998. *Quick Activities to Build a Very Voluminous Vocabulary*. New York: Scholastic.

Nomura, Y. 1985. *Pinch & Ouch: English Through Drama*. Tokyo, Japan: Lingual House.

Nuemann, S. 1999. "Books Make a Difference." *Reading Research Quarterly* 34: 286–310.

Ohman-Rodriguez, J. 2004. "Music from Inside Out: Promoting Emergent Composition with Young Children." *Young Children* 59: 46–49.

Opitz, M. F. 1995. *Getting the Most from Predictable Books*. New York: Scholastic.

———. 2007. *Don't Speed. READ! 12 Steps to Smart and Sensible Fluency Instruction*. New York: Scholastic.

Opitz, M. F., and M. Zbaracki. 2004. *Listen Hear! 25 Effective Listening Comprehension Strategies*. Portsmouth, NH: Heinemann.

Opitz, M. F., and T. V. Rasinski. 2008. *Good-Bye Round Robin*. Updated ed. Portsmouth, NH: Heinemann.

Orellana, M., and A. Hernandez. 1999. "Talking the Walk: Children Reading Urban Environmental Print." *The Reading Teacher* 52: 612–19.

Ovando, C. J., and V. P. Collier. 1985. *Bilingual and ESL Classrooms: Teaching in Multicultural Contexts*. New York: McGraw-Hill.

Palmer, B. C., and M. A. Brooks. 2004. "Reading Until the Cows Come Home: Figurative Language and Reading Comprehension." *Journal of Adolescent and Adult Literacy* 47: 370–75.

Penfield, J. 1987. "ESL: The Regular Classroom Teachers' Perspective." *TESOL Quarterly* 21: 21–39.

Peregoy, S. F., and O. F. Boyle. 2008. *Reading, Writing, and Learning in ESL: A Resource Book for Teaching K–12 English Learners*. 5th ed. Boston: Pearson.

Reutzel, D. R., P. Hollingsworth, and J. Eldredge. 1994. "Oral Reading Instruction: The Impact of Student Reading Development." *Reading Research Quarterly* 29: 40–62.

Robinson, F. P. 1946. *Effective Study*. New York: Harper.

Roller, C. 1996. *Variability Not Disability*. Newark, DE: International Reading Association.

Sampson, M. R., R. V. Allen, and M. B. Sampson. 1991. *Pathways to Literacy*. Chicago: Holt, Rinehart and Winston.

Saricoban, A., and E. Metin. 2000. "Songs, Verse and Games for Teaching Grammar." *Internet TESOL* 6: 10.

Scarcella, R., and R. Oxford. 1992. *The Tapestry of Language Learning: The Individual in the Communicative Classroom*. Boston: Heinle and Heinle.

Schifini, A. 2006. "Bonding Words." Retrieved from www.languagemagazine.com /december2006/vocab_strat_dec06_LM.pdf.

Schinke-Llano, L. 1983. "Foreigner Talk in Content Classrooms." In *Classroom Oriented Research in Second Language Acquisition,* ed. H. W. Seliger and M. H. Long, 146–64. Rowley, MA: Newbury House.

Schreiber, P. A. 1980. "On the Acquisition of Reading Fluency." *Journal of Reading Behavior* 12 (3): 177–86.

Shanahan, T., and I. Beck. 2006. "Effective Literacy Teaching for English Language Learners." In *Developing Literacy for Second Language Learners*, ed. D. August and T. Shanahan. Mahwah, NJ: Erlbaum.

Smith, F. 1986. *Joining the Literacy Club*. Portsmouth, NH: Heinemann.

Snow, C., M. Burns, and P. Griffin. 1998. *Preventing Reading Difficulties in Young Children*. Washington, DC: National Academy Press.

Stauffer, R. G. 1975. *Directing the Reading-Thinking Process*. New York: HarperCollins.

Stipek, D. 2002. *Motivation to Learn: Integrating Theory and Practice*. 4th ed. Boston: Allyn & Bacon.

Swan, M., and B. Smith. 2001. *Learner English: A Teacher's Guide to Interferences and Other Problems*. London: Cambridge.

Templeton, S. 1991. *Teaching the Integrated Language Arts*. Boston: Houghton Mifflin.

TESOL. 2006. *PreK–12 English Language Proficiency Standards*. Alexandria, VA: Teachers of English to Speakers of Other Languages.

Topping, K. 1987. "Paired Reading: A Powerful Technique for Parent Use." *The Reading Teacher* 40: 608–14.

Tracey, D. H., and L. M. Morrow. 2006. *Lenses on Reading: An Introduction to Theories and Models*. New York: Guilford.

Vacca R., and J. Vacca. 2008. *Content Area Reading*. 9th ed. New York: Allyn & Bacon.

Vogt, M., and J. Echevarria. 2008. *99 Ideas and Activities for Teaching English Learners with the SIOP Model*. Boston: Pearson.

Vygotsky, L. S. 1978. *Mind in Society. The Development of Higher Psychological Processes.* Cambridge: Harvard University Press.

Ulanoff, S. H., and S. L. Pucci. 1999. "Learning Words from Books: The Effects of Read-Aloud on Second Language Vocabulary Acquisition." *Bilingual Research Journal* 23: 409–22.

Wilhelm, R. W., G. Contreras, and K. A. Mohr. 2004. "Barriers or Frontiers: A Bi-National Investigation of Spanish-Speaking Immigrant Students' School Experiences." Paper presented at the Annual Convention of the American Educational Research Association, April, San Diego, California.

Wood, K., J. Flood, D. Lapp, and D. Taylor. 2007. *Guiding Readers Through Text*. 2d ed. Newark, NJ: Erlbaum.

Woodbury, J. 1979. "Choral Reading and Readers Theatre: Oral Interpretation of Literature in the Classroom." In *Developing Active Readers: Ideas for Parents, Teachers, and Librarians*, ed. D. L. Monson and D. K. McClenathan, 65–72. Newark, DE: International Reading Association.